Rev. Charlene West ⬚⬚⬚⬚⬚⬚⬚⬚⬚⬚⬚⬚⬚⬚⬚
describes her own lif⬚⬚⬚⬚⬚⬚⬚⬚⬚⬚⬚⬚⬚
She takes incidents from her life to teach spiritual ⬚⬚⬚⬚
for triumphant living. Charlene West's ministry as pastor
in Oklahoma and California, missionary to Costa Rica and
Venezuela has made a tremendous impact for the kingdom
of God. She has recently planted *Centro de Celebración* in
Oklahoma City where she continues to pastor.

Presiding Bishop James D. Leggett
International Pentecostal Holiness Church

Life Is a Great Adventure should be required reading in mis-
siology and theology for all Bible college students! If the
words "Great" and "Adventure" can be used to describe the
life of any one person, that would be Rev. Charlene West.
From her early days as the wife of a Pentecostal pastor, to
the moment of assuming the leadership of a large congregation upon her husband's sudden death, to her twenty-two
years as a missionary to Costa Rica and Venezuela, to the
decision to leave a full-time ministry position at the age
of sixty-eight to plant what is today a large, prosperous,
Hispanic Church in Oklahoma City, the life of this outstanding preacher, teacher, church planter, pastor, and missionary has been driven by passion, commitment, sacrifice, and
anointing. Her potential was never dictated by her situation
but by the revelation of God's will abiding deep in her heart.

Dr. Ronald Carpenter
Director of Evangelism USA
International Pentecostal Holiness Church

It was my privilege to meet Charlene West over thirty years ago. Her passion for God and His Word was evident; so was her passion and love for people. This deep passion has kept her spirit aflame and enlarged her circle of influence that now reaches around the world. She is a mother and example of godly womanhood who has walked in integrity and wisdom throughout the years; she is an excellent role model for women who sense the Holy Spirit calling them to a deeper level in ministry. Charlene West has led the way as a church leader, teacher, apostle, prophet, evangelist, and pastor, and done so with excellence. It is my joy to heartily commend her and this book to you!

Jewelle E. Stewart
Executive Director, IPHC Women's Ministries
President, Evangelical Women Leaders of the NAE

To

Dr. Frank and

Lu

Life is a Great
Adventure

Thanks for your
beautiful ministry!

Charlene West

Life is a Great *Adventure*

Discovering Truth in the Journey of Faith

CHARLENE H. WEST

TATE PUBLISHING & *Enterprises*

Published by Tate Publishing & Enterprises, LLC
127 E. Trade Center Terrace | Mustang, Oklahoma 73064 USA
1.888.361.9473 | www.tatepublishing.com

Tate Publishing is committed to excellence in the publishing industry. The company
reflects the philosophy established by the founders, based on Psalm 68:11,
"The Lord gave the word and great was the company of those who published it."

Book design copyright © 2007 by Tate Publishing, LLC. All rights reserved.
Cover design by Luke Southern
Interior design by Lindsay B. Behrens

Published in the United States of America

ISBN: 978-1-60462-164-8
1. Christian Living   2. Spiritual Growth   3. Inspiration   4. Motivational
07.11.20

This book is lovingly dedicated:

To my family;
To those who have shared with me in
the work of the Lord;
To my spiritual children begotten in the ministry;
And to you, who will read these pages and
perhaps learn or be refreshed
by some of the tremendous truths I found as
I traveled the highway of
Life's Great Adventure.

Life's Adventure

Life is a great adventure,
And those who care to win
Have faith in God that makes the weakest
Walk with lifted chin.

Faith that tunnels through the mountains,
Faith that sails uncharted seas,
Faith that trusts in God and others,
Faith that's born on bended knees.

Faith that will not be defeated,
Faith that holds a vision clear,
Faith that hurdles each obstacle,
Faith that laughs at doubt and fear.

Faith that sees what is invisible,
And counts it now as done,
Faith that believes that all is possible,
Faith that knows all battles won.

Charlene H. West

Table of Contents

Note

Songs Daddy sang were mostly a ballad type, and I have not seen them in print.

Poems were written by the author, Charlene West, with the following exception:

Stevenson, Robert Luis, *A Child's Garden of Verses*, "My Shadow" and "The Swing." William Morrow and Company, Inc., New York City, NY, 1998.

Introduction

My small grandchildren used to climb up on my lap, and their requests were nearly always the same: "Grandma, tell us a story." I told stories like those about the three little pigs, but more often than not, they were true stories from the Bible. Other favorites, however, were those real-life ones to which they could relate. The girls' common requests were, "Tell us about when Mama was a little girl," and, "Tell us about when you were young."

Let's see. How shall I begin? "Once upon a time, there was a girl named Charlene, and for her, life became a great adventure...." I've told many of you parts of this story over and again; yet there are lots of things I've never shared. I must admit, however, that I'm not very fond of just talking about myself. As I have ministered the Word from the pulpit or on an individual basis, I have usually been inspired to share my experiences as illustrations. I have hoped that they could serve as windows to let God's light shine on some truth about which I was teaching or preaching.

So my prayer is that each segment of this story may just be an illustration of biblical truth. That is the only way I can justify the time and effort of this undertaking. Spiritual realities have accompanied each phase of my life, and I want to share them with you as I continue. Theological issues have shaped my life, and my responses to them have anchored me on the Solid Rock. These tremendous truths have served as guiding lights on the journey of my life with Christ, and I hope they will be a blessing to you. Come along! Life is a Great Adventure!

Birth

Charles North, affectionately called "Charlie," was expectantly waiting for the pending news of the delivery of his third child. He and Bertha already had two girls, Gertrude and Evelyn. They were healthy kids; whenever he sat down, they were all over him with hugs and kisses. It would have been impossible to love anyone more that he loved his little girls.

But this time he was hoping for a boy. He was from an ancestral line of preachers. His father, although long retired, was a preacher; an older brother was the pastor of a church in Texas. It was only natural that he, too, would like to have a preacher-son to follow in his footsteps. A sense of quiet penetrated his thoughts as he realized that the groans and sounds of pain from the other room had stopped. His new baby's adventure in life had just begun!

Dr. Smith appeared to give him the news. "Congratulations, Preacher. All is well, and you've got another healthy little girl!" Charlie soon held the little bundle in his own arms. What would they call her? "Had you been a boy, your name was all picked out. You would have been 'Charles.' But now you're a little girl, and what shall we call you?"

"Well, Charlie," Bertha suggested from the bed, "this is our third. What if we don't have any more? Let's go ahead and name her after you. We could call her Helen Charlene."

"No, let's make it Charlene Helen. Since I'm Charles Henry, she'll have my initials. She's just a little package of possibilities now, and so much will depend on how we bring her up. We'll just believe the Lord to make her into what He wants her to be for His glory. I know you'll make me proud of you, little one, and you'll honor my name. Yes, you will be Charlene Helen–not Helen Charlene."

Who would guess that Dr. Smith, with a part of his mind likely on other things, would only hear the last part—Helen Charlene—and put that on the register of live births. But she was Charlene Helen on all her legal documents. Only years later, when she got a copy of her birth certificate to apply for a passport, did she learn the truth. Dr. Smith had put her name down backwards!

How important is your given name, your ancestral line, or the circumstances surrounding your birth, for that matter? The Bible has quite a lot to say about these things. In fact, our ancestral line is very much a part of the message of salvation! As far back as I can remember in my journey of life, I heard the plan of salvation. I accepted as truth everything Daddy preached, because he backed up what he said with verses from the Bible.

First of all Daddy emphasized the importance of love. "You know I love you," he would say, even though he needed to correct us. His love was always constant and continually evident. "And, remember, God loves you, too."

Then there was a second step in the gospel message we heard. It was that sin separated us from God, because "all have sinned and come short of the glory of God" (Romans 3:23). Daddy told us all about how it started in the Garden of Eden as Adam started out on his adventure of life.

Adam was the very first man, the head of the whole human race. He was created in God's image and likeness, and God gave him everything he could want in his paradise garden. He even gave him a wife to stand at his side. He also gave Adam authority over his entire world—the birds, the animals, and the fish of the sea. Adam was subject only to God, his Creator. To prove that Adam accepted his authority, God asked for his strict obedience in one specific thing.

> And the Lord God commanded the man, saying, "Of every tree of the garden you may freely eat: But of the tree of the knowledge of good and evil, you shall not eat, for in the day that you eat of it, you shall surely die."
>
> Genesis 2:16, 17

The command was short, clear, and easy to understand. Later God gave Adam his wife, and Adam must have repeated to her God's order, because she understood completely and could easily repeat the command.

Then one day Satan appeared to Eve and caused her to question what God had said. "Just look at the fruit of this tree. It's good to eat! You won't die; in fact, your eyes will just be opened so that you will be wise—like God!" So the woman listened, and she looked. It did indeed look delicious. How wonderful if it would make her wise like God! She and Adam wouldn't need to depend on Him so much.

Maybe Eve had been skirting around this tree—just staying away from it. But now she listened to the Tempter and took a good look at the fruit.

> And when the woman saw that the tree was good for food, that it was pleasant to the eyes, and a tree to be desired to make one wise, she took of its fruit and ate. She also gave to her husband with her, and he ate.
>
> Genesis 3:6

Now this sounds like a very simple little story, but Jesus, as well as Eve, faced these areas of temptation. John in his first letter warns us about the same things and deals with three global passions or desires: the lust of the flesh, the lust of the eyes, and the pride of life (1 John 2:16). He warns us that everyone confronts these temptations.

Notice how Satan tempted Eve by bringing doubt on God's word. "Has God indeed said…?" (Genesis 3:1). He also tried to make Jesus doubt. Jesus had just come from his baptism in water and had heard God say from heaven, "This is my beloved Son in whom I am well pleased" (Matthew 3:17). Satan attacked the truth of this statement and tempted Jesus to negate the very affirmation God had just given him by saying, "If you are the Son of God…." Jesus, however, knew how to confront the enemy, and in this portion of scripture, he gives us the secret of victory over temptation. He just shot back another truth at him from Scripture: "It is written …" (Matthew 4:4).

The first temptation had to do with the lust of the flesh. In Eve's case, it was something that looked good to eat—fruit. In Jesus' temptation, it also had to do with eating. He had fasted forty days and was hungry; the enemy appealed to that basic physical need. Satan came and said, "If you're really the Son of God, you don't need to be hungry. Just turn these stones into bread!" (Matthew 4:3). Could Jesus have satisfied his hunger in this way? Yes, of course! He later multiplied the loaves and fish. Not everyone can do this, however, and Jesus won the victory over Satan as a man and not as God. Eating, we know, is not the only passion of the flesh. There are the strong passions or desires for drugs, alcohol, tobacco, illicit sex, etc. Jesus, as our divine example, showed us the way to use our weapon against the enemy by saying, "It is written, Man shall not live by bread alone" (Matthew 4:4).

The second temptation mentioned came through the sense of sight. The enemy spoke, and Eve listened and looked. The woman saw that the tree was good for food, [and] that it was pleasant to the eyes …" (Genesis 3:6). The enemy was programming her to doubt God and then to dis-obey Him. He confronted Jesus in the same way. "The devil took him up on an exceedingly high mountain, and *showed him* all the kingdoms of the world and their glory" (Matthew 4:8). The kingdoms of this world are serving Satan; he told Jesus that he would give them all to Him if he would fall down and worship him. Jesus again shows us the way to victory by saying, "It is written, You shall worship the Lord your God and Him only you shall serve" (Matthew 4:10).

The third temptation John mentions has to do with the pride of life—fame, the desire to be recognized, and the passion to receive the applause of others. The tempter told Eve that this fruit would make her wise—that she would become like God (Genesis 3:5). The devil also said to Jesus, "Why don't you just float down from this pinnacle of the temple into the patio. All of those people standing down there will applaud you as somebody really great" (Matthew 4:6). Then he added Scripture to his attack; he backed up his temptation with the very word of God! "If you're the Son of God, you won't fall, because it is written, He gives his angels charge over you, and you won't even dash your foot against a stone" (Matthew 4:6). The enemy knows the Scriptures, and he will use them against you. At an early age, I learned to use this tremendous sword against the enemy in life journey.

Eve yielded to the enemy in each of these temptations, but Jesus was victorious. Jesus has already assured your victory! The Apostle Paul declared that in everything "we are more than conquerors through Him who loved us" (Romans 8:37). Maybe the little chart that follows will help you remember these truths as you fight your battle against Satan. You can win the victory over every temptation in life's great adventure with Christ!

1 John 2:16; Genesis 3:1-6; Matthew 4:3-11

Lust of the flesh (John)
Good for food (Eve)
Stones to bread (Jesus)

Lust of the eyes (John)
Pleasant to the eyes (Eve)
Showed him the kingdoms (Jesus)

Pride of life (John)
Desired to make one wise (Eve)
Float down from the temple (Jesus)

Who was guiltier, Eve or Adam? The Bible clearly says that Eve sinned because she was deceived (1 Timothy 2:14). She may not have personally heard God's instructions since she was given to Adam after he received them. She belonged to Adam and was under his protection to love, instruct and guide. Adam should have cancelled out her disobedience and brought her back into her rightful relationship with the Creator. What Adam should have done was later made clear under Mosaic Law. It speaks of the woman who makes a vow.

> If indeed she takes a husband, while bound by her vows or by a rash utterance from her lips by which she bound herself, and her husband hears it, and makes no response to her on the day that he hears, then her vows shall stand, and her agreements by which she bound herself shall stand. But if her hus-

band overrules her on the day that he hears it; he shall make void her vow which she took and what she uttered with her lips, by which she bound herself, and the Lord will release her.

Numbers 30:6–8

Adam could have been Eve's kinsman redeemer. He was *with* her! He could have said, "No, no, Eve! Don't do that! The consequences are too great!" But he did nothing to stop her. In fact, when she gave the fruit to him, he ate it in willful disobedience to God's clear command.

There were immediate consequences of their disobedience. They had been clothed with God's glory, but now sin made them destitute of that precious covering. They realized that they were naked, and their hearts were throbbing with guilt. They tried sewing fig leaves together to cover their nakedness, but it was useless. Man can never cover his sins with what he can do. God's Word clearly declares that our salvation is a gift of God and "not of works, lest anyone should boast" (Ephesians 2:9). Adam and Eve, who had walked with God and enjoyed his fellowship, now hid from him. God, however, loved them, and called them back into his presence to face the consequences of their rebellion. Adam would have to earn his food by the sweat of his brow among the thorns and thistles that would grow; Eve, under subjection to her husband, would bear children with great pain and suffering. They were both cast out of the Garden and separated from God's presence. They no longer had access to the tree of life, for no man or woman walking in disobedience can enjoy the blessings of eternal life. Instead of life, they chose death. Instead of obedience to God, their Creator, they chose submission to Satan, God's enemy. The authority God had given to them passed into the hands of the Deceiver. Instead of the divine spiritual connection with God they had enjoyed, there was the emptiness and void of spiritual death. And that is what they have transmitted to every person in their ancestral line! The Apostle Paul puts it like this: "Therefore, just as through one man sin entered the world, and death through sin, and thus death spread to all men because all sinned" (Romans 5:12).

But did Adam really die because of his sin? Did Satan tell the truth when he told Eve, "You shall not surely die" (Genesis 3:4)? To answer this question, one must understand what is meant by death. There are three types of death: physical death, spiritual death, and eternal death.

It must be understood that none of these brings about a cessation of existence but a separation that has to do with the triad of man's being as spirit, soul and body (1 Thessalonians 5:23).

1. The *body* is the house or habitation of the spirit and soul. It makes contact with our surroundings through our five senses: sight, hearing, smell, taste, and touch.

2. The *soul* is the person who lives in the body; it houses the will, emotions, and intellect. It makes us conscious of who we are as individuals. The soul tells us that the body belongs to him/her when it says, "*My head* hurts," or "*My body* is strong." It is not separated from the spirit but keeps its identity with the spirit when they leave the body.

3. The *spirit* is the part of us that is conscious of God through conscience, instinct, and perception. It is the breath God breathed into Adam to make him a living being. The spirit and soul leave the body together and will be taken to a place of rest if they die in Christ, or to torment if they reject Him (John 3:36; Revelation 20:11–15).

The death of the body is called physical death and takes place when the soul and spirit leave the corporal home. One moment the organs in the body are functioning, and then something happens. Some vital part fails to work and the action of the body stops. The organs are still present, and the whole body is there to be seen, but it cannot move. There are eyes, but they cannot see; ears, but they cannot hear; a mouth, but it cannot speak. We say that person is dead; deterioration immediately sets in. With time the body returns to the dust from which it was taken until that day when the dead shall arise—some to everlasting life and some to shame and everlasting contempt (Daniel 12:2).

Spiritual death reigns in a person whose *soul* and *spirit* have no connection with God. That person may be in excellent physical health, but the separation of the soul and spirit from the Creator means he is spiritually dead. All of Adam's children have inherited spiritual death and don't have to do anything to get it. They are born with Adam's fallen nature: "For by the offense of one judgment came upon all men to condemnation" (Romans 5:18). Anyone outside of Christ is spiritually dead; this inherited sin-nature becomes a source of sinful actions.

So again, we confront the question: Did Adam really die? God had said, "In the day you eat of it, you shall surely die" (Genesis 2:17). Adam certainly didn't experience *physical* death that day. In fact, Genesis 5:5 says, "So all the days that Adam lived were nine hundred and thirty years; and he died." How then could God have fulfilled his word?

What Adam experienced the day he sinned was *spiritual* death, because he lost his spiritual connection with God. God confronted Adam and pronounced judgment upon him and his wife. He even clothed them with the skins of animals, which in reality happened again when Jesus died on the cross—an innocent victim died so that the guilty sinner could be covered from his sin and shame.

Adam's separation from God is graphically illustrated in his expulsion from the Garden of Eden, his paradise home. He would never return there, for God placed cherubim with a flaming sword that turned every way "to keep the way of the tree of life" (Genesis 3:24). Yes, Adam died. Instead of fellowship and peace, he had guilt. Instead of God's glory, he was destitute of his holy covering and clothed with the skins of animals. Instead of the verdant green of Paradise, he was removed to a desert growing with thorns and thistles. Instead of a daily walk with God in the cool of the day, he toiled in the heat of the wilderness. And with time, Adam also died physically.

It is natural for a person to want to leave an inheritance for his children. We usually think of an inheritance in terms of material means. But many people consider their spiritual inheritance, such as godly teachings and a good example to follow, more important than material wealth. They remember that "a good name is rather to be chosen than great riches, and loving favor rather than riches and gold" (Proverbs 22:1).

But what an inheritance Father Adam left his posterity! As the head of our race, he left us his fallen, sinful nature and every one of us has been affected. God's Word says that "… through one man's offence judgment came to all men resulting in condemnation" (Romans 5:18).

The Bible mentions Adam repeatedly. It speaks of Adam's sin, his "old nature," his transgressions, the condemnation and curse he brought upon us, and Scripture tells us that "all die" in Adam. I'm not very proud of the inheritance Father Adam left me!

My earthly father, on the other hand, left me a wonderful heritage. I don't count my inheritance in terms of earthly wealth, because what I have inherited is much more basic and permanent than material possessions. I must thank him for leaving me a good name. I was always happy when someone said, "Oh, you are one of the North girls!" Then, there was the godly example. Daddy traced out a path that I could follow. He was there to give me counsel and encouragement—to help me grow and develop in my Christian experience. More than anything else, Daddy left me an appreciation and love for God's Word. He was ever a great student himself and an avid reader of other great preachers. We discussed together the Scriptures, and he always gave me answers that satisfied.

I will be happy if my children can say these same things about me when they analyze the inheritance I leave behind. Let's pause at this point and ask ourselves what kind of inheritance we are leaving our children. But don't stop long, because we must move on! After all, we're on a Great Adventure!

Innocence

Mary and her mother were visiting the parsonage. I was supposed to be sharing my toys, but when Mary picked up my favorite doll, I grabbed it and said, "Mine!" Wise parents begin the process of teaching their children as soon as they are born. I can remember the do's and don'ts of early childhood. "Be sweet to little sister." "Don't play with matches; you might start a fire." "Be nice and quiet in church."

I learned to obey the rules, but I didn't understand the concept of the sin and guilt that come from disobedience. When I was punished for doing something wrong, the punishment was soon over and I was back at play again. The old nature I inherited from Adam, however, was evident—I could disobey, be angry, scream, and cry, but in a little while I forgot all about it. Even now as I look back, I can hardly remember feeling guilty about anything I did. I was living in an age of innocence.

The future of children rests greatly on what we teach them in the early formative years of their innocence. Children learn the norms we set up and understand what we say. They know the meaning of the word, "No!" (If *we* really mean it). Children can also appreciate the affirmation we give them when they do what is right and, above all, the assurance that we love them. If we don't correct them when they are disobedient, we start a losing game. It is when a child, in these early years, has the right kind of teaching that he is best prepared to meet the temptations he will confront later in life.

Is a child saved or lost during this time? Is he too young to receive the Lord? What if he dies? Should we baptize our children? A statement of Jesus clears up this doubt for us. "Let the little children come to Me, and do not forbid them; for of such is the kingdom of God" (Mark 10:14). Until children come to an age of understanding about what disobedience and guilt are, they have no sins to confess. They are already a part of God's kingdom. They may repeatedly come forward to receive Christ as Savior even though they don't really understand what being saved means. Don't forbid them. Each step toward Christ is a step in the right direction.

It is important to present your children to the Lord as Jesus was when he was taken to the temple when the days of Mary's purification were accomplished (Luke 2:22–24). There is no merit, however, in baptizing a new baby. Infant baptism is not Christian baptism. In Acts 8:37, Philip lays down the requirement for Christian baptism. Water baptism requires a statement of faith that a person has received Jesus as Lord. A baby can't even talk, much less make such a statement of faith. He must reach an age of accountability or understanding of what sin, guilt, and forgiveness mean in order to be saved or baptized in water. For some children accountability comes at an early age.

We don't know how long Adam and Eve lived in a state of innocence before they fell for Satan's lies and disobeyed God. They were created without sin and knew no sin or guilt until they were confronted with temptation and fell. Eve could repeat God's instructions and tell exactly what would happen if they disobeyed, but with temptation her intellect took over. Reason said, "Why don't you just give it a try and find out for yourself?" She and her husband both ate of the forbidden fruit and died spiritually, because they were separated from their fellowship and communion with God their Creator. That event marked the end of their age of innocence. The road they followed took a new turn that day in their journey of life.

One young lady, in the agony and pangs of childbirth, said to me, "Just look at what Eve brought on us. If I ever get the opportunity, I'm going to ask her *why* she did it!" Such a statement makes reflection necessary. Eve, coming out of her innocence, met the tempter and fell. What did *you* do when you first became conscious of your sins? On one hand the temptation called, yet on the other Jesus said, "I love you. Come and follow me." Every one of us has had a "Garden of Eden" experience. We, too, confront what Adam and Eve faced. Either we fall for Satan's invitation to sin, or we declare our fidelity and obedience to God and receive Jesus as Lord of our lives. Our response to that temptation is the critical moment when we move out of the age of innocence and into another arena of life.

I was born in 1930, the year after the financial crash of '29. That event rocked the very foundations of the U.S. economy and started a depression that would affect our entire nation for several years. People lost their fortunes over night, many committed suicide, banks closed, mortgages on homes were foreclosed, and hungry people stood in lines just to get a meal. Our congregation was small and the people were not affluent. Daddy's salary as a pastor depended on what came in through tithes and offerings and, of course, the "poundings." Poundings were the non-financial offerings for the pastor—eggs, milk, fruit, garden vegetables, and sometimes a chicken or fresh meat if someone butchered. Poundings would be on the dining room table after the church service was over. Even though money was scarce and the financial resources of the people were limited, Christians rejoiced and shouted the victory. Daddy preached and sang; people prayed, and God blessed.

It was a blessing that Mother was a good seamstress. Flour came in printed cotton sacks in those days, and two twenty-five-pound bags were turned into a pretty little dress. Clothes were also handed down to us from the member's kids and from one sister to another. I remember having a nice little gray coat with a red flower on the shoulder. Mother had expertly cut around the worn places on one of Daddy's old suits, and—*voilá!*—it was transformed into something entirely different: a classy-looking little coat for Charlene! Mother wanted us to look our best, and when we went to church and lined up on the pew, we looked pretty good with our long curls.

I was just six, but I'll never forget the Christmas of '36. The Stationing Committee had moved us from the church in Oklahoma City to one in Ponca City. (It was a step up the ladder for Daddy, and the parsonage was much better than what we were used to.) The Christmas tree in our home was lit up with a unique string of lights—one light was an old frog, one a Santa, and one a snow-covered little cottage, among others. In his spare time, Daddy was busy at something on the back porch, and no one was allowed to even peek. Mother was also sewing secret things. On Christmas morning, Daddy blew a toy horn and declared that old Santa had arrived. (We knew, of course, who Santa really was!)

We tumbled out of bed, and sure enough, lined up under the tree was our big surprise. Orange crates had furnished the wood to build a doll bed with slats for each one of us. Mother had made the miniature mattresses, pillows, and bedclothes, and had also fashioned the clothes for each doll lying on its little bed.

Just a week later, God granted Daddy what he had always longed for—a son. Our little brother Gerald was born, and we all thought he was the most wonderful thing that ever happened. He came on the last day of the year bringing a lot of joy into the home as 1936 was just about to slip away into the past. In just a little over three months, however, tremendous changes would take place. In the journey of life we traveled, we came upon an unexpected turn of the road.

Daddy had a dream. He saw Mother on the other side of a ditch. It was wide, and he couldn't seem to cross over and get to her. At this point of frustration, he woke up. The dream had seemed very real, and it disturbed him. What did it mean?

Mother took a cold that went down into her chest, and the congestion just refused to break up. We believed and practiced divine healing, but Daddy was never against the medical profession, so he called the doctor. "It's pneumonia," the doctor said. "We need to get her to the hospital and under oxygen." The ambulance came, and she waved to us from the stretcher as she left. Then a real fight for her life began. People fasted and prayed; medical science pulled out all the stops, and the doctor did all he could. But in those days there were no antibiotics, and penicillin hadn't yet been discovered. So Mother slipped across the great divide; Daddy understood the meaning of his dream. They came from the funeral home and put a wreath on the parsonage door.

"Precious in the sight of the Lord is the death of his saints," the church people wept as they quoted Psalm 116:15. Grandma and Grandpa Russell and her siblings came and wept. "She was a saint," they said. Everyone wept. "She was a saint," they said. Family, loved ones, and friends crowded into the little white-framed building for the funeral, and the minister read the obituary, "Her stay on this earth was twenty-nine years, three months, and twenty-six days." He said she was a beautiful Christian, a good wife and housekeeper, and a wonderful mother. "She was a saint," he concluded.

The ladies trio, from the church Daddy had pastored in Oklahoma City, sang: "I will meet you in the morning, just inside the Eastern Gate." The power of the Holy Spirit swept low over the congregation and filled that little building with God's presence assuring us that she had made a victorious entrance into that land of eternal day. She was laid to rest in Longwood Cemetery on the outskirts of Ponca City.

Daddy had to make immediate decisions. Oscar Moore, a long-time friend and fellow-minister, who later became General Superintendent of our denomination, talked to Daddy. "Charlie, you know that Ana and I don't have any children. Let us have Gerald. We'll take him, educate him, and give him a good home."

But Daddy was adamant about one thing: his children would not be separated from each other, and they would not be separated from him. How was he to keep the home with five children, ranging from three months to eleven years old, and still do his work? Aunt Dink, Mother's sister, stayed a while, but she was very young. A young couple from the church who had no children stayed for a while, but it was a very temporary arrangement. Grandma North, who was now elderly, came for a while, but I think we were probably just too much for her. She was a little childish, and I distinctly remember that she was partial to me.

One day, after doing some shopping she said, "Here, I've brought all of you something," and she gave each one a piece of candy. "But Charlene, look, I've bought *you* a little broom. You can help Grandma with the housework!"

Things just weren't the same. "I hate to do this," Daddy said as the scissors took off our curls, "but I just can't take care of your hair." We drew hopscotch on the walk to entertain ourselves, played jacks, and hobbled on tin-can walkers, but I distinctly remember another time-killer. Just across the field was the train track; we counted the cars to see if this one was as long, or longer, than the last. Tremendous pastimes! As far as I know, television hadn't even been dreamed of in those days.

I always thought Daddy was a handsome man, and some single ladies evidently thought so too, even if five kids did go with the package. Daddy knew that remarriage had to be the logical solution to his problems at home—problems that couldn't be separated from his pastoral ministry. But he would do his own choosing!

"Charlene, you can go with me. I'll leave you in Oklahoma City, and pick you up as I come back from a place called Carnegie." It was a very cold winter day and, although the heater in the car worked, cold air seemed to whistle in through the cracks and crannies. Daddy settled me in the front seat with him, and covered me from my waist down with a quilt, especially wrapping my feet to keep them warm. Then he put a little book in my lap.

"This is a little gift for you," he said, "you can read to me as we travel." *A Child's Garden of Verse* it said on the cover, by Robert Luis Stevenson. By now I was in the third grade and a pretty good little reader.

"I have a little shadow," (I read)
"That goes in and out with me.
And what can be the use of him
Is more than I can see …"

On through the little book I read…

"Oh, how I love to go up in a swing,
Up in the air so blue.
Oh, I do think it's the pleasantest thing,
Ever a child could do …"

Daddy encouraged me to read, and I learned that I could travel the world and visit fascinating places through books. I could experience the excitement of rubbing shoulders with kings and queens living in castles. I might even marry a prince and live happily ever after!

I didn't realize it the day of that trip, but Daddy's mission was to find us another mother. Life really is like a trip, and we are fellow travelers on a tremendous mission. Let's move on with it! After all, life really is a Great Adventure!

Born Again

Daddy married Audie Hill, a widow with two daughters. Wanda was just six months older than I was, and we would be in the same third-grade class at school. Doris was a year-and-a-half younger. Daddy called us all together and gave us a good talk.

"This is your new mother. You will mind her as you did your own mother; you will respect her, and do what she tells you. You are to be good, and you are not to fuss and fight with each other." We heard and obeyed—when we were under their watchful, eagle eyes. Even among children, however, conflicts not experienced before the parents' marriage may build up, resentment often finds a place in the heart, and unkind words may be spoken.

"We've got a revival scheduled with Rev. Lonnie Smith," Daddy announced to the church. "Let us be much in prayer that God will save the lost, sanctify the believers, and fill everyone with the Holy Ghost." It was a Godsend, especially for the parsonage family. Lonnie Smith was almost like a relative—sort of an uncle. We liked his preaching, even though his voice was a little raspy. His delivery was enthusiastic and under the anointing of the Holy Spirit. His invitations to accept Christ were sincere and compelling.

"Step out from where you are. Kneel down at this old-fashioned altar. Lay the burden of your sins at the feet of Jesus, and receive him as Lord of your life."

It was the children who began to respond—of the preacher's children there were Evelyn, Wanda, Doris, and me. Gertrude, our oldest sister, wasn't ready yet; Betty and Gerald were too young. The treasurer's kids came forward, and the deacon's too. "Let the little children come unto me," Jesus said, "and forbid them not, for of such is the kingdom of God."

That night I got saved. But upon what basis could I establish that declaration of faith? Perhaps I didn't understand theologically what was involved, but several things were important to me:

First, I realized that I was a sinner. Although I was only seven years old, I knew I had done naughty things and needed forgiveness. I also understood that nothing I could possibly do would be sufficient to buy my salvation. "For by grace you have been saved through faith, and that not of yourselves; it is the gift of God, not of works, lest anyone should boast (Ephesians 2:8, 9). Grace meant that God loved me, even though I didn't deserve it.

Jesus knocked on the door of my heart that night and told me through His Word that if I would open the door, He would come in and be with me always. I understood that He carried my sins to the cross and died to pay the penalty of death that was pronounced upon Adam. It was my responsibility, however, to accept personally what Jesus did for me.

"Believe on the Lord Jesus Christ, and you will be saved," the Bible assured me. "Repent," said Peter on the Day of Pentecost. "If you confess with your mouth the Lord Jesus, and believe in your heart that God has raised him from the dead, you will be saved" (Romans 10:9), Paul wrote to the people in Rome. So that night, I received Jesus into my life with just a simple prayer:

> Thank you, Father, for your Son, Jesus, who took my sins to the cross. Please forgive me for all the things I have done to displease you. I invite you to come into my heart, and I ask you to save me. I accept you as my Savior and Lord of my life. Thank you, Lord Jesus. Amen.

I had done what God told me to do, "for with the heart one believes unto righteousness, and with the mouth confession is made unto salvation" (Romans 10:10). I now knew that I belonged to God. In fact, the Bible said that I was a member of His family—one of His children (John 1:12; 1 John 3:1, 2).

Daddy wanted us to grow in our new experience of being born-again, and it helped to have a family altar at home. He would always read a short scripture and then lead us in prayer. Mom and Dad would call out our names, asking God to protect us and keep us from the evil of the world. We would leave the parsonage and head for school with their blessings ringing in our ears. Daddy was giving us, as newborn babes, the sincere milk of the word and was guiding us in our newfound walk with Christ.

Aren't we supposed to be baptized in water? "Yes," Daddy explained, "water baptism is a command of Christ." He himself was baptized in water as an example for us to follow. He commands us to be baptized, and we must be obedient to him in all things. But water baptism doesn't save us. Do you know why? It is an important ceremony and is an outward testimony of what has happened in your life, but it is administered by man. The only basis for our salvation is what *Jesus* did for us. Then we begin to obey the Lord in all that we do and that, of course, includes water baptism.

One Sunday afternoon in March, we went to the river for a baptismal service (our church didn't boast a baptistery in those days), and I shall never forget that the water was exceedingly cold! I was shivering! There we were, a bunch of kids (some adults, too) confirming with this outward testimony what we had experienced inwardly. Over each one of us, Daddy lifted his hand to heaven and declared, "Upon the confession of your faith in Christ as your Savior, I baptize you in the name of the Father, and of the Son, and of the Holy Ghost."

Daddy explained that going under the water represented our death to the old life and that coming up again was a sign that we were to walk in a way pleasing to the Lord. "Therefore we were buried with Him through baptism into death, that just as Christ was raised from the dead by the glory of the Father, even so we also should walk in newness of life" (Romans 6:4). Thus we gave public witness to what God's divine grace had made a reality in our hearts.

We had another baby brother. Charles was born when I was eight. Daddy sometimes said we were a family made up of his kids (five), Mom's kids (two), and their one. Eight children, and with Mom and Dad, we were ten! We had to sleep three in a bed, and all the elements for chaos were present, but I guess we got along pretty good.

It was hardest on Gertrude. Mom and Dad would visit the sick and needy, and leave us in her care. Conflict would begin when she would lock us all out so that she could clean the house. She would sweep, mop, run the vacuum, and dust, but when our parents came home there was an outcry! "She made us stay out in the heat! She wouldn't let me in for a drink of water!" Those were problems the parsonage family had to solve. But the revival really did change the atmosphere in the parsonage, and those of us who got saved tried to act as Christians should. We no longer fussed or fought because that was Daddy's decree, but because God had wrought changes in our lives.

"You are just as saved if you wake up sick as when you feel great," Daddy said, "because you are not saved by your feelings. You have accepted Jesus into your life; God's Word declares that you are saved, and you have believed it. Always remember that you are saved because of what Jesus did for you, and not because of any work that you may have done."

"'Not by works, lest any man should boast,'" Daddy said. Well, in the parsonage there was always plenty of work, and everybody had to do their part. We made up our own beds, put up our clothes, picked things up, and took turns doing dishes. We worked in two teams, three per team: one member of the team would clean off the table and put up the food, another washed, and the third dried the dishes and put them up. No team wanted Sundays, Thanksgiving, or Christmas, so we rotated. We were so good at washing dishes that sometimes a member of the church hired a couple of us to do her dishes after a big company meal. She would get a real bargain—she usually paid us about a quarter to clean the kitchen stacked full of dirty dishes!

There was also work related to canning vegetables and making jams, jellies, and pickles. People gave us garden vegetables, or Mom bought produce by the bushel at the Farmer's Market. We shelled mountains of peas and washed mountains of fruit jars. "Charlene, this is a good job for you. Your hands are small, and they will go right down into those jars. I know you'll get them nice and clean." Works! I understood that while works didn't save us, we would be rewarded or judged by them. I surely hoped that washing fruit jars and shelling peas would count!

Although I had settled the question of works, there was another issue that puzzled me. Some kids from another church said that certain people were predestined to be saved and that others were predestined to be lost. I had never heard of what they were talking about, and I wanted to know what this predestination meant.

"Well," Daddy said, "the truth of the matter is that God had us in His plans and purposes from the very beginning. His Word tells us that 'He chose us in Him before the foundation of the world, that we should be holy and without blame before Him in love' (Ephesians 1:4). That is His predestination for us. He chose all of us to be for his glory! We've talked a lot about Adam, and how we were 'in him' when he sinned. To help you understand that better, let me just ask you a simple question. I am your father, but if I had died when I was a little boy, where would *you* be?"

"Well, I wouldn't *be!* You wouldn't have had any children when you were a little boy, and I certainly couldn't have been born without my father!"

"You're right, of course. You were 'in me' when I was a boy, and had I died, you would have died in me. If we keep tracing our family tree back, we get to Noah, then on back to Adam who sinned and fell. But guess where Adam was before he came into being? He was in the creative work of God! In fact, before I was in Adam by human birth, I was in God by creation! That is the reason why the eternal Son of God was the only being in the entire cosmic universe who could save the human family from Satan's ruin. God had said, 'The soul that sins will die.' Since that judgment was passed on *man*, God's Son had to become a man to pay the penalty for all of us. Only in Jesus could the past, present, and future be embodied. When he went to the cross, He carried in Himself every person who was born, or would be born, of Adam's race along with all this groaning creation. God had pronounced judgment and said, 'The day you sin, you will die!' Jesus, His only Son, took our sins and their penalty upon Himself, and when he died and said, 'It is finished,' we were in Him and died. The penalty for sin was paid for every one of us. That is why by just 'one offering' he could pay the debt for all humanity (Hebrews 10:14).

"So, Charlene, if we believe that *all* of us died spiritually in Adam, the head of the human race, by the same token we must believe that all of us live in Jesus, the head of the new race, because He cancelled our sins when He died on the cross. In 1 Corinthians 15:47–49, the Apostle Paul tells us about Adam, the first earthly man, and Jesus, the second heavenly man.

> The first man was of the earth, made of dust; the second Man is the Lord from heaven. As was the man of dust, so also are those who are made of dust; and as is the heavenly Man, so also are those who are heavenly. And as we have born the image of the man of dust, we shall also bear the image of the heavenly Man.
>
> 1 Corinthians 15:47–49

Another verse of that chapter says, 'And so it is written, the first Adam was made a living soul; the last Adam was made a quickening spirit' (1 Corinthians 15:45, KJV). So as all are lost in the first Adam, all are saved in the second Adam—if we make the decision to accept what the second Adam did for us.

"There is no 'limited' salvation, and no one is predestined to be lost. Jesus paid the price for everyone at the same time, and salvation is available for each and every person. 'For God so loved the world that He gave his only begotten Son, that whoever believes in Him should not perish but have everlasting life' (John 3:16). God's Word tells us that it is not His will that 'any should perish, but that all should come to repentance' (2 Peter 3:9)."

"Daddy, I understand that Jesus paid the price for every person, and that *each one of us* must choose our own destiny by either accepting or rejecting what Jesus did when He cancelled our debt of sin. I made the decision to accept what Jesus did for me, and I have already read what John 3:16 says. That if we believe, we have *everlasting* life. Does 'everlasting' mean it is impossible for me to be lost? My friends said that once we were in grace we would always be in grace [or in God's favor], and that we could never lose our salvation. Is that true? Is that what the Bible says?"

"Jesus gives us a very interesting comparison in John 15. Let's look at verses 5 and 6. 'I am the vine, you are the branches. He who abides in Me, and I in him, bears much fruit; for without Me you can do nothing. If anyone does not abide in Me, he is cast out as a branch and is withered; and they gather them and throw them into the fire, and they are burned.' Jesus was talking to his followers—those who were saved. You see, you have eternal life because Jesus lives in you. He is eternal and cannot die. You were not saved until you invited Jesus to come into your life and dwell there. God has made you a part of His family through His Son, Jesus Christ. If you then separate yourself from Him, these verses tell you what will happen.

"Remember that Adam and Eve willfully separated themselves from God. As a result, they were cast out of the Garden so that they could not eat of the Tree of Life and live forever. They must already have been eating of that Tree and enjoying eternal life, since only the tree of the Knowledge of Good and Evil was forbidden. But when they sinned, they lost access to the spiritual life God had given them.

"Just as the dried, withered branches in John 15 were cast into the fire, so the Bible tells us that 'anyone not found in the Book of Life was [or will be] cast into the lake of fire' (Revelation 20:15). The Apostle Paul himself warns us of becoming a castaway. 1 Corinthians 9:27 says, 'But I discipline my body and bring it into subjection, lest when I have preached to others, I myself should become disqualified.'

"Some people will tell you that once you have made a decision and your name has been written in the Book of Life, it will always be there. But Jesus says in Revelation 3:5 that it is those who overcome whose names are found in that Book. 'He who overcomes shall be clothed in white garments, and I will not blot his name out of the book of life.' The logical conclusion, of course, is that if you do not overcome, if you put your hand to the plow and look back, your name *can* be blotted out. This principle was very clearly taught in the Old Testament.

> When the righteous turns from his righteousness and commits iniquity, he shall die because of it. But when the wicked turns from his wickedness and does what is lawful and right, he shall live because of it.
>
> Ezekiel 33:18, 19

"God loves us and goes to all means to bring us into fellowship with Him. He will use His Word, the pastor, evangelist, other believers, and different circumstances of life to bring us to Him. But the choice is ours. I am so glad you have made a firm decision to live for Jesus. The Bible warns us and tells us to live in fellowship with God at all times and to be obedient to Him. The same people who tell you that you can never be lost will also tell you that you are always a sinner and that you sin every day in word, thought, or deed. That is not Bible language, Charlene. Bible language is what Paul says in Romans 6:1 and 2. 'Shall we continue in sin that grace may abound? Certainly not!' John also writes and tells us, 'My little children, I write to you, so that you may not sin.' If we do something wrong, however, we must not give up, but immediately take that to Jesus and ask Him to forgive us and restore our relationship with the Father."

These were all questions I asked Daddy over a period of time. He discipled me and answered the many questions that came up from time to time, and it all started that night there in Ponca City when I gave my life to Jesus.

"How was the revival?" someone asked a long-faced church member. "Well, it was mostly just a bunch of kids," he responded.

But many years of my journey with Christ have now passed, and I can still remember the names of that "bunch of kids" who were not only children of the pastor but also of the deacons, treasurer, and other members of our congregation. In fact, most of us have had some contact with each other through the years. Not only were our souls saved, but our *lives* were saved and made to count for Christ. With time, all of us kids became faithful members and leaders in the church—musicians, Sunday school teachers, deacons, preachers, and ministers in different areas of God's harvest. Some have gone on now to be with the Lord, but as far as I know, not one has fallen by the wayside and been lost.

As I traveled the path with Jesus, I learned to follow Him, and I had godly examples around to help me on the way. I found that God was able to keep me from falling as I walked with Him. I met other people dedicated to Christ who were traveling the same highway. It seemed to me that they had words of encouragement, a clap on the shoulder, or a smile just when I needed them most. On this journey, of course, I never knew what I was going to encounter around the next bend of the road. I learned one thing, however, if I walk with the Lord, life really *is* a Great Adventure.

Crucifixion

In those days, our church services always included a "testi-mony" time. The saints (that's what the Bible calls believers) always testified to being saved, sanctified, filled with the Holy Ghost, and looking for the soon-coming King. The songs, sermons, and testimonies always let people know our doc-trines of faith! The testimonies were supposed to be short, to the point, up-to-date, and follow on the heels of another testimony. If the in-between pause got too long, Daddy would pick up his guitar and sing a song to liven things up. Everyone loved to hear him sing "The Sanctified Life."

> I'll sing you the song of a sanctified life,
> A life set apart from all sin.
> A beautiful life free from envy and strife.
> Where Jesus is dwelling within.
> Where Jesus is dwelling within,
> He's keeping my soul calm and clean.
> A beautiful life free from envy and strife.
> Where Jesus is dwelling within.
>
> One night while communing with Jesus quite late,
> He whispered this message to me,
> Despised and rejected outside of the gate,
> I suffered to sanctify thee...

Sanctification is also called the "second blessing," because it takes place after a person is saved. God had very definitely sanctified Daddy, so he could freely sing about this experience:

> Since then I've been marching with triumphant tread,
> Through Canaan's rich fruit-bearing clime,
> For self has been slain, and the "old man" is dead,
> And victory is mine all the time.

Was I sanctified? How was that different from being saved? Daddy was really good about giving answers I could understand. "When you received Jesus as your Savior, you told him you were sorry for your sins—those naughty things you had done. You were responsible for those things, so you confessed them to the Lord, and He forgave you and saved you. But, Charlene, there is still that nature of sin you were born with. You don't have to ask to be forgiven for that, because you are not responsible for it. You inherited it from Adam."

Wow! Here's Adam again. He lived centuries and millenniums ago, and he just keeps on popping up! People "in Adam" do what they don't want to do, practice what they hate, and don't do what they know they should. How could I ever get rid of Adam?

I shall never forget an incident when that old Adam thing worked in me to do something I still sincerely regret. Betty, my younger sister, was following our group of older girls, and I turned and shouted, "Go back home!" And I threw a rock. It hit Betty on the forehead just above her eyes, and she started bleeding. That broke up our party. We all ran back to the house, and I had to confess that I was the guilty one. Daddy attended to Betty, and still he looked at me with compassion. He said all that was necessary, because he saw how sorry I was. "You know, you might have put out her eye." I didn't do that, but Betty still carries a little scar to remind me of the need to let Jesus control all that I am and do.

"A war goes on," Daddy said, "between that old nature you were born with and the new nature you received in Christ. Before the new nature comes in, the old carnal nature does everything he wants to do. You have to get rid of it."

Some people teach that you are sanctified and get rid of this old nature when you die. They believe that the death of the person does away with the carnal mind. But this kind of sanctification is of no benefit to those of us who live now! Paul was speaking to born-again believers when he said, "Now the God of peace Himself sanctify you completely; and may your whole spirit, soul, and body be preserved blameless at the coming of our Lord Jesus Christ. He who calls you is faithful, who also will do it" (1 Thessalonians 5:23, 24). Paul, in his letter to Titus, also instructed Christians that "denying ungodliness and worldly lusts, we should live soberly, righteously, and godly in the present age, looking for the blessed hope and glorious appearing of our great God and Savior Jesus Christ" (Titus 2:12, 13). So sanctification is for us today, in this present age—in the here and now! Your death can't sanctify you, only the death of Jesus can accomplish that!

Others believe that you are sanctified after you die, but that you go to a purgatory where you will suffer for the sins you committed here on earth—sins you didn't ask forgiveness for before you died. After this purging, you will then be ready to go to be with the Lord. [There is no reference to such a place in the Bible.] While the Bible teaches us that a sinner does go to a place of torment, it definitely says that there is no way for him to get out. When the rich man, who died and went to Hades, wanted Lazarus to come and put a drop of water on this tongue, Abraham answered back, "Between us and you there is a great gulf fixed, so that those who want to pass from here to you cannot, nor can those from there pass to us" (Luke 16:26). Paul taught that death for a Christian is just a step into the world to come. For him to be absent from the body was to be present with the Lord (2 Corinthians 5:8). If we have not prepared to meet the Lord before we die, we are specifically told that there will be no other opportunity.

Some believe that you are sanctified when you are saved, and that after you are saved sanctification is just a process of your growth and maturity as a Christian. But if you are diseased with an "old Adamic nature," how can you grow a healthy life until you are healed of that terrible malady? The disciples were certainly not sanctified when they believed. Although they were followers of the Lord, and their names were "written in heaven" (Luke 10:20), they were still bickering over who would sit next to the Lord and who would be greatest in the Kingdom. Jesus knew what their need was, and in his high, priestly prayer in John 17, he specifically prayed that they might know the joy of victory over sin and sinning.

> Sanctify them by Your truth. Your word is truth. As you have sent me into the world, I also have sent them into the world. And for their sakes I sanctify Myself, that they also may be sanctified by the truth. I do not pray for these alone, but also for those who will believe in Me through their word; that they may be one, as you, Father, are in Me, and I in You; that they also may be one in us, that the world may believe that you sent Me.
>
> John 17:17–21

Sanctification is a work of the Spirit (Romans 15:16), and it may be that the disciples received this experience when Jesus breathed on them and said, "Receive the Holy Spirit" (John 20:22). At any rate, by the Day of Pentecost this experience had become a reality in their lives, because they were all in one place and *in one accord!* (Acts 2:1) Jesus' prayer for their sanctification had become a reality. Although we see differences of opinion on certain occasions later, we do not see the manifestation of that old nature any more.

Well, the Apostle Paul gives an illustration using the home of Abraham and compares it to our heart. Abraham thought he could help God fulfill his promise to give him a son by having one by Hagar, his wife's slave girl. This son, Ishmael, grew year by year; it seemed he was going to inherit everything his father Abraham had. All was going his way, and he did everything he wanted to do. But a tremendous event took place when Ishmael was fourteen years old. Abraham and his wife, Sarah, had a son of their own.

Ishmael, who was born by the flesh and not by promise, represents the carnal life and its desires. Isaac was born in fulfillment of God's promise and symbolizes the Christ-life that has come into your heart as a result of the new birth. Isaac and Ishmael lived in the same home for some time, but there was constant conflict because of the two children. One day Sarah caught Ishmael making fun of Isaac, and she made up her mind. She went to Abraham and said something like this: "Get rid of that slave girl and her son. I can't stand to have them in our home keeping this conflict going! Her son is not going to be heir along with our son, Isaac" (Galatians 4:30). Notice that the war didn't begin in the home until the son of the promise came in, and the war didn't stop until Ishmael was cast out! (He certainly would not have *grown out* as he matured. He would only have grown stronger and more dominant!)

You have a human nature with basic needs and drives for food, clothing, shelter, learning, desire for posterity, and self-fulfillment. The carnal nature we inherited from Adam seeks to pollute and deviate these natural desires until they are transformed into such things as gluttony, adultery, drunkenness, homosexuality, idolatry, envy, anger, etc. Long lists are given in Galatians 5:19–21 and Romans 1:24–32, as well as other places in the Bible. People who live the old carnal life according to Adam's nature give free reign to these expressions.

According to Galatians 5:22–23, the sanctified life of the spirit results in love, joy, peace, long suffering, kindness, goodness, faithfulness, gentleness, and self control. The next verse goes on to say that "Those who are Christ's have crucified the flesh with its passions and desires (Galatians 5:24). So the question before us is: "How can this crucifixion take place in my life?"

We are saved because Jesus took our *sins* to the cross and paid the penalty for them, and we are sanctified because He carried that *old nature* to the cross. "Knowing this, that *our old man* was crucified with Him [Christ], that the body of sin might be done away with [destroyed, KJV], that we should no longer be slaves of sin" (Romans 6:6). So the provision was made for us to be freed from our sins (actual transgressions) and also from that inherited sin nature we got from Adam. Some call this a "double" cleansing, and James talks about it in his letter. "Cleanse your hands, you sinners; and purify your hearts, you double-minded" (James 4:8). God always call sinners to repentance and believers to holiness. Just as we are saved by a definite act of faith upon accepting Jesus as Lord, it takes a definite act of faith on our part to be sanctified. We are told exactly how to take this step of faith:

> Likewise you also, *reckon yourselves to be dead indeed to sin,* but alive to God in Christ Jesus our Lord. Therefore do not let sin reign in your mortal body, that you should obey it in its lusts. And do not present your members as instruments of unrighteousness to sin, but present yourselves to God as being alive from the dead, and your members as instruments of righteousness to God. For sin shall not have dominion over you...
>
> (Romans 6:11–14, *emphasis added*)

When we hand over the old nature and declare it "crucified with Christ," we enter into a new position in Christ. The Apostle Paul experienced this "crucifixion" and witnessed to it in Galatians 2:20 (KJV). "I am crucified with Christ; nevertheless I live; yet not I, but Christ lives in me; and the life which I now live in the flesh I live by the faith of the Son of God, who loved me, and gave himself for me." When Paul wrote that "our old man *was* crucified" with Christ (Romans 6:6), he used the past preterit of the "to be" verb (*was*). It is a one-time action that is over—was crucified—once and no more. "By one offering, he has perfected forever them that are sanctified" (Hebrews 10:14, KJV). In Galatians 2:20, however, the phrase, "I *am* crucified," is a present continuous tense that indicates a *position* to be held.

I had a very definite experience of sanctification when I was ten years old. Until that time, I just lived for the Lord as a child and followed Him as I knew how. But knowledge of the Word brings us to experience, and one night, as the Spirit moved in the service around the altar, the Lord sanctified me. In that service, He put a brand new love in my heart for the Lord and for other people.

1. Salvation
2. Sanctification

1. Position: Child in God's family
2. Position: Freed from sin

1. The New Birth
2. Crucified with Christ

When I was saved, I became a child in God's family. That was my position through the new birth. When I was sanctified, I was freed from the old nature through death—*I am crucified with Christ!* Each of these positions is held secure because Christ lives in me. Willful sin is the only thing that can affect my position in Christ.

"Daddy, I was reading in the Bible that Barnabas determined to take Mark with him and Paul on their second missionary journey, but Paul wouldn't let him go because Mark had left them on their first missionary trip. And it says that 'the contention became so sharp' that they separated. Barnabas took Mark to Cyprus, and Paul took Silas. Do you think Paul and Barnabas were sanctified?"

"Yes, they just had different opinions. Both wanted what was best for God's work, and they based their opinions on their understanding of the situation. Paul felt that Mark was disqualified because of his previous action, but Barnabas believed in giving him a second opportunity to go forward. [In fact, Barnabas had helped Paul get a second chance to go forward by inviting him to minister with him in Antioch!] Barnabas also may have wanted to help Mark because he was his nephew."

"Who was right? Do we know?"

"Well, we know that Paul and Silas were commended to the grace of God by the leaders of the church in Antioch. The account of their journey is in the Book of Acts. They visited the churches previously started and founded new ones, in spite of such tremendous problems as beatings, imprisonment, and stoning. God blessed their work and confirmed His Word through them with healings and miracles."

"What happened when Barnabas and Mark went to Cyprus? What about Mark? Did he continue to work for God?"

"We don't have a biblical account of what happened in Cyprus, but we know that Mark later became a worker alongside the Apostle Peter. In fact, Peter calls Mark his son (1 Peter 5:13). No doubt as Peter talked about his time and experiences with Jesus in his earthly ministry, Mark determined that Jesus' story should not be forgotten. So he wrote the first gospel account of Jesus' life, and it is found as the second book of the New Testament. Do you remember what that is?"

"Certainly! The Gospel of Mark! Was he the Mark that Paul didn't want to take? *That* Mark?"

"That's right! Maybe Paul's decision not to take Mark made that young man determine to make his life count for Christ. Perhaps he decided that from then on, he would never do things halfway! There's another detail of interest about Mark, though. Many years later, when Paul was in prison in the city of Rome, he wrote to Timothy: "Get Mark, and bring him with you, for he is useful to me for the ministry" (2 Timothy 4:11). I think this sort of tells us that over time, Paul was able to change his original opinion about Mark. Mark had proven himself.

"Charlene, one door of ministry was closed to Mark, because a church leader didn't feel that he qualified for the task at hand. Yet God opened other doors for Mark to excel in his ministry. Always believe the best of your leaders. If one seems to close a door to you, God will see to it that another opens if you maintain the right attitude. Really the disagreement of these two great men worked out for the advancement of God's work. As Christians, we sometimes disagree because we don't have all the information. God's Word says that we just know in part. Being sanctified doesn't mean that we are glorified! That will come on the Day of Resurrection when our bodies become immortal, and when that which is perfect has truly come.

"We've talked about sanctification as a definite, critical experience. That's when we present ourselves to God as a living sacrifice that is holy and acceptable [Romans 2:1] to Him for service. This experience, however, is to be followed by our daily walk of holiness. You know Peter calls us a 'royal priesthood.' Of course, the priests all had to be born into the family line of Levi. You and I also, in order to belong to the 'royal priesthood,' must experience a new birth into God's family! When the time came for the priests to begin their priestly duties, there was a consecration ceremony that began with a ceremonial washing."

> Then you shall bring Aaron and his sons to the door of the tabernacle of meeting and wash them with water. You shall put the holy garments on Aaron, and anoint him and consecrate him, that he may minister to Me as priest.
>
> Exodus 40:12, 13

This initiation was never repeated, but every day as the priests went into the Holy Place to minister, they passed the brazen fount where they were to stop and wash their hands and feet. The floor of the tabernacle was the sand of the desert, so as they went about their duties their hands and feet became soiled. Similarly, as we go about our daily walk, we need to stop and ask God to cleanse us anew. We must take time for reflection and renewal before our Lord so that we may be fit to minister to others in His name

This means that it isn't enough just to say the Lord sanctified me on a certain date, but to understand that we must daily keep our position of commitment to Christ. Paul not only said, "I am crucified with Christ," he also said, "I die daily" (1 Corinthians 15:31). God's standard for the Christian is holiness, and he says that we are to follow peace with all people and "holiness, without which no one will see the Lord" (Hebrews 12:14). God Himself spoke, "You shall be holy, for I am holy" (Leviticus 11:44).

Some people think holiness is just what you do, how you look, and what you wear. As I grew up in the church, I followed the norms without any problem. In those days, we didn't go to movies—not even the Shirley Temple ones. Today we can have videos of what they showed in the theatres back then, but the Hollywood movie industry is corrupt; if we have movies as our entertainment, we must chose with discretion. Women and girls didn't wear pants, either, because that was being dressed in men's clothing. We didn't even wear the little leggings that came with some of the winter coats—they were called "snow suites" and the pants and coats matched. As time went on, I had to learn that outward holiness, while necessary, had nothing to do with fashion. It meant that I was to reflect Christ in all that I was as well as what I wore. Styles change, but God's principles of modesty abide. Some people rebel and swing the wrong way. Others just learn that wherever you are, as you live and work—even out there in the world—there will be norms and, at times, dress codes to obey. If we learn to follow godly leaders, we will learn well! I make no apologies for those days. I learned to follow God back then.

It is necessary that we be holy, for we are in warfare against an unholy enemy. The Apostle Paul, however, tells us that "the weapons of our warfare are not carnal but mighty for pulling down strongholds" (2 Corinthians 10:4). A time came when the Christian people of our nation learned to do spiritual warfare on a global level against a very human and carnal enemy.

We were living in Oklahoma City, and Daddy was pastoring our church on Agnew Street. I was eleven years old and in the sixth grade at Columbus Grade School when a national crisis came to our country. It happened on Sunday, December 7, 1941. We had been in Sunday school and worship service that morning. In the parsonage, Mom had added mashed potatoes, English peas, cole-slaw, yeast rolls, and a quick cake to the pork roast that had been cooking while we were assembled in the church. She was an excellent cook—no one could cook like Mom! We had eaten that typical Sunday meal and were doing the typical mountain of dishes that followed. Then, something unusual happened. The radio was tuned to the "Old Fashioned Revival Hour," but a voice broke in and said, "This program is being interrupted. Stand by for a special announcement." All of us just froze as we listened. The Japanese had bombed Pearl Harbor, interrupting the Sunday calm of the Hawaiian beach with a series of bombs falling from a flight of warplanes. One after another, our ships sank in the harbor, and our nation went into mourning.

The next day an announcement came over the intercom in our homeroom class. The pupils of the fourth, fifth, and sixth grades were to meet for a special assembly in the auditorium. We would hear a declaration of war by radio, and I can still hear the voice of President Franklin D. Roosevelt when he said, "I hate war!" Yet he declared war against the Japanese, Germany, and Italy.

The news always seemed to come on while we were eating our evening meal. The radio had usually been turned off during mealtime, but now things were changed. It was left on, but unheeded, until that moment when Dad would say, "Okay, kids, listen! The news is on!" We heard reports of defeat and victory, gains and terrible losses. Nations had already fallen under the onslaught of Adolph Hitler, cities were reduced to rubble, and Great Britain stood almost alone. The U.S., Russia, and Great Britain became the Big Three of the Allied Nations (with fifty nations finally joining in the fray). In the U.S., our young men enlisted and hardly a family existed without some member in the military service.

People were mobilized to win the victory. Moms left their household duties to the kids and took jobs left vacant by the men who had joined the service. I was now at Jackson Jr. High, and every homeroom competed to see which class could bring in the most scrap metal. We cut out both ends of the canned goods and flattened the cans to take to school. Gasoline was rationed. Necessity is the mother of invention, and oleo margarine came on the market to replace the heavily rationed butter. It wasn't anything like what we have today. It was a white block with a little envelope of color to add. I'll say Mom was inventive on this one! She softened it, squeezed in the color, added some Milnot (a substitute for canned milk), beat it with the electric beater, and *behold!* We had a spread we could at least look at as we spread it on the biscuits!

We were at war and people pled before God's mercy seat for their sons and other relations. God blessed the church in those times of crises. One night Daddy was about to play the guitar and sing while people prayed around the altar when Charles, barely school age, scooted up to him and said, "Daddy, sing 'Comin' in on a wing and a prayer!'"

That war came to a victorious conclusion. Hitler committed suicide on April 30, 1945; on May 7, Germany surrendered unconditionally to the Allies, ending the war in Europe. On August 6 and 9, we dropped atomic bombs on Hiroshima and Nagasaki, respectively. On August 14, Japan agreed to surrender unconditionally and signed the terms of surrender aboard the U.S.S. Missouri in Tokyo Bay on September 2, 1945.

But another global war rages on today. A tremendous conflict seeks control of the souls of men, women, youth, and even children. Satan is dedicated to steal, kill, and destroy. Jesus, on the other hand, declares, "I have come that they may have life, and that they may have it more abundantly" (John 10:10). He died that we might live.

Many of our boys never came home from the battlefields of Europe, the South Pacific, and other parts of the global conflict. They died to save people from the exterminations by Hitler and the conflict of submarine warfare. We won World War II at a great cost, but it doesn't compare with the cost of our salvation from eternal slavery to Satan, sin, and death. Victory is costly, but so is defeat. In Christ our victory is already won! In Him there is no defeat! Believe it! Proclaim it! Declare it! Shout it!

We are more than conquerors in every battle as we travel this journey on our Great Adventure with Christ!

Resurrection

I was saved and, after I had been "buried with Christ" in water baptism, understood that I was raised to walk in newness of life—resurrection life! The Bible tells me it is the Holy Spirit who makes possible this life of resurrection power.

> But if the Spirit of Him who raised Jesus from the dead dwells in you, He who raised Christ from the dead will also give life to your mortal bodies through His Spirit who dwells in you.
>
> Romans 8:11

This scripture not only anticipates the day when our mortal bodies shall be changed into immortal ones, but it also tells us that the change will take place because the Spirit of God dwells in us.

"Just remember, Charlene," Daddy said, "that the Holy Spirit is the agent who brings into reality the work God does in your life. In the first chapter of Genesis, the Spirit brooded over our planet—which was dark, empty, and void—and brought about a new creation, just as He initiates God's work in your life. The Spirit works in different dimensions."

1. Before salvation
2. Salvation
3. Sanctification
4. Baptism of the Holy Spirit

1. Reproves and convicts of sin
2. Witnesses the new birth
3. Separates, cleanses
4. Fills, seals, equips for service

1. John 16:7–11
2. Romans 8:16
3. Romans 15:16
4. Acts 2:4

This explanation helped me see how the Holy Spirit could work in different stages of a person's life. I could see that many people, and even denominations who taught a born-again experience with the Lord, just walked in a salvation experience. Others moved on into a life of holiness, but they stopped short of a life in the fullness of the Holy Spirit.

Ezekiel saw levels in the life-giving waters that Daddy talked about. They flowed from under the threshold of the temple, and they were certainly spiritual waters of divine origin. The prophet saw a man move into them to his ankles (Ezekiel 47:3). He was not really bathing—just wading! So the Holy Spirit comes first just to deal with us about the way we live and walk. God knows us and brings to our attention our sins against Him. It is the Holy Spirit who reproves, convicts, and convinces us to ask Jesus to forgive us of our sins, accept Him as Lord of our lives (John 16:7–11), and change the way we live. Conviction of sin is not salvation; it just prepares us for it!

And so if we want to make spiritual progress on life's journey, we must wade on out into the waters that are up to our knees (Ezekiel 47:4). Kneeling before God is an indication of surrender to Him. As we accept Jesus into our lives, it is the Holy Spirit who "bears witness with our spirit that we are children of God" (Romans 8:16). Being born again is a new birth of the Spirit, as Jesus explained to Nicodemus (John 3:5–6).

A journey with the Lord always means progress, so Ezekiel saw the man go on out into waters up to his waist (Ezekiel 47:4). He had now reached a level of water where he could wash and be clean but still keep his feet on the ground. It is logical and necessary to wash ourselves from the things of the world, and God uses the waters of the Holy Spirit to bring about our experience of sanctification.

> Husbands, love your wives, even as Christ also loved the church and gave Himself for her, that He might sanctify and cleanse her with the washing of water by the word, that He might present her to Himself a glorious church, not having spot or wrinkle or any such thing, but that she should be holy and without blemish.
>
> Ephesians 5:25–27

There is another dimension of the Spirit in which the prophet saw the water become a river. "The water was too deep, water in which one must swim, a river that could not be crossed" (Ezekiel 47:5). In the previous areas of the Spirit, the believer can have his feet on the ground of spiritual understanding, but when he moves into the *river* of the Spirit, his feet no longer touch the bottom. He must move into another dimension—a sphere of the supernatural—where he can no longer reason with human logic.

Our life in this dimension of the supernatural begins with what the Bible calls the "baptism of the Spirit." Jesus said, "For John truly baptized with water; but you shall be baptized with the Holy Spirit …" (Acts 1:5). He instructed his followers not to leave Jerusalem, but to wait for the promise of the Father—the Holy Spirit—that He had already told them about (John 14:16, 17, 25, 26; 16:7–14).

We don't know how many people heard these words, but when the Day of Pentecost came, just ten days after the day of Jesus' ascension, His followers gathered in an Upper Room. Among those present were the eleven, Mary (Jesus' mother), and his brothers—who were by then convinced of Jesus' divinity. In addition, other women and followers of the Lord were present. Jesus had told them all to wait for the promise of the Father.

The Day of Pentecost was one of the seven major feast days of Israel—a time of feasting and celebration in the city of Jerusalem. As those in the Upper Room prayed and worshipped, something astounding happened!

> Suddenly there came a sound from heaven, as of a rushing mighty wind, and it filled the whole house where they were sitting. Then there appeared to

them divided tongues, as of fire, and one sat upon
each of them. And they were all filled with the Holy
Spirit and began to speak with other tongues, as the
Spirit gave them utterance.

Acts 2:3–4

"Filled with the Holy Spirit" is an expression that often
reminds me of the different dimensions of the work of the
Spirit in a Christian's life. I have compared having the Spirit
in my life to a glass with water in it. It can have just a little
bit in the bottom, but still water is there. It can be one-third
full or even three-fourths full; when it is *really filled,* just a
drop will cause it to run over. And that is the kind of experience God wants us to have—one that is sufficient—not just
to meet our own needs, but one that can spill over and bless
others. David said, "My cup runs over" (Psalm 23:5), and
Paul said, "Be filled with the Spirit" (Ephesians 5:18).

I remember when my sister Evelyn was baptized in the
Spirit. She was ten years old. She praised the Lord in other
tongues with her eyes closed and danced in the Spirit all
over the sanctuary. That convinced some who were there
that this was without doubt a valid experience. What child
would invent such a thing?

Until I was thirteen years old, I just walked in a salva-
tion/sanctification experience; I don't remember really having been urged to move on into the fullness of the Spirit.
Then Daddy preached a revival in Yukon, Oklahoma. After
his message on Sunday night, we gathered around the altars
to seek the Lord. I didn't go forward with the intention of
being filled with the Spirit, but Daddy passed by me and

said, "Charlene, you can be baptized in the Holy Spirit tonight! Just look right up and be filled to overflowing." Suddenly, I began to praise the Lord and the praises began to well up from within me. As I worshipped, my English praises were changed into new words I had never heard before. I was speaking in other tongues! I had been baptized in the Holy Spirit!

Speaking in the tongues of the Spirit is something entirely different from speaking any other language. As a high school student, I opted for a college prep course, which included a foreign language class. I decided to take Spanish; I still look back and praise the Lord for my teacher, Mae Sackett. She was well ahead of her times with her emphasis, not only on reading and writing, but also on listening and responding. I was learning a new language and Daddy was my sounding board at home. He was my *Papá* who read off my vocabulary lists in English while I wrote them down in Spanish. It was hard work. Miss Sackett said: "Don't ask if you have homework. You always have homework except at Thanksgiving, Christmas, and Easter holidays." Through our textbook *El Camino Real,* we got a good workout through the stories we read, portions we had to translate, vocabulary to learn, along with the spelling lists, pop quizzes, and exams. I finished those two years of Spanish wishing I could have studied the language another year!

Speaking in the language of spiritual tongues, however, is something entirely different. You don't get it by taking classes or learning vocabulary. It is a supernatural gift and flows out from the inner core of your being. When I received the baptism of the Holy Spirit, I received this heavenly language of prayer and praise. It made me continually conscious of the fact that the Spirit had come to "abide with me forever."

People and churches that believe in the baptism of the Holy Spirit and speak with tongues are referred to as Pentecostals because they practice what happened in the Upper Room on the Day of Pentecost. It never occurred to me to doubt the validity of this experience, because as the old timers used to say, "I was rocked in a Pentecostal Holiness cradle." I also knew it was a biblical doctrine solidly founded on God's Word. For me, sanctification is a definite experience, but I learned that many who received this blessing believed that their experience of sanctification was the baptism of the Holy Spirit. Why should they then seek God for something they already had? So I learned that not everyone believed in the baptism of the Holy Spirit as we did. Some thought it was fanaticism, some called us "holy rollers," and many looked down on us. Many felt that speaking in tongues was just a lot of jabbering.

"Daddy, it's right there in the Bible. Why can't they see it? How do they excuse themselves for not believing? Do they just ignore the Scriptures?"

"Well, they can't really cut those scriptures out of their Bibles. They just explain them away."

"How do they do it? It seems to me that everyone ought to want something that is as wonderful as this powerful experience that God has provided!"

"Well, Charlene, some say that when you are saved and receive Christ as Lord, you also receive the Holy Spirit and that salvation includes everything. The new birth is a spiritual birth and we don't deny the work of the Holy Spirit in our salvation. Many have been taught that when they receive the Lord, they are "complete" in Christ (Colossians 2:9, 10), and that any additional 'experience' is unnecessary."

The "partly-true" positions are the most often misunderstood. When Jesus died, was buried, resurrected, and ascended, he *did* make provision for everything. We were "in him" by creation when He went to the cross. But we already know that while the new birth is available, it is not actually in our lives until we *experience* it through the confession of our faith in Jesus. This is true of everything we receive from God.

The Holy Spirit works in every spiritual dimension into which we enter. He is the Agent who executes in us God's eternal purposes. When we receive Christ, the potential for every other spiritual blessing exists (Ephesians 1:3). But if we want to *experience* these blessings, we must take hold of each one by faith; only then may they become realities in our lives.

Some quote Ephesians 1:13 and teach that when a person is *saved,* he is "sealed until the day of redemption." Therefore, the believer has everlasting life and will always be saved. In fact, they would never be lost. This gives people a mistaken sense of security, leading them to think that in spite of the way someone lives after confessing Christ as Lord, that person is eternally saved. I have been to many funerals when the minister affirmed to a suffering family that their loved one was now in the presence of the Lord— this in spite of the fact that, although in some remote past that person had made a confession of Christ as Lord and had been baptized in water, he hadn't darkened the door of a church in years. He had lived *like* the world *in* the world, had not witnessed of God's saving grace in his life, nor had he been a part of the Lord's work. We must be aware of what God says through the Prophet Isaiah: "But your iniquities have separated you from your God; and your sins have hidden His face from you, so that He will not hear" (Isaiah 59:2). Unless we are overcomers in this life, our names can be "blotted out" of the book of life (Revelation 3:5).

Let's read Ephesians 1:13 and just consider what that sealing of the Holy Spirit is. "In Him you also trusted, *after* you heard the word of truth, the gospel of your salvation; in whom also, *having believed,* you were sealed with the Holy Spirit of promise" (NKJV, *emphasis mine*).Some versions however, instead of the preposition "after," substitute the word "when" in translating this text, putting this "sealing" into another possible time frame. Notice how this scripture is translated in the following versions:

- KJV   *after* that you believed, you were sealed
               Modern Language have as *believers in*
               Him been sealed

- J B Phillips *after you gave your confidence to Him* you
               were, so to speak, stamped

- NAS   *having also believed,* you were sealed

These scriptures indicate to me that believing came first and the sealing came afterward. What does the Bible say about this timing? The Samaritans: The Holy Spirit had fallen upon *none* of them. The Ephesians: Did you receive the Holy Spirit *when* you believed? No, we haven't even *heard* of the Holy Spirit! It was after a correction of their doctrine and their baptism in water that Paul laid his hands on them and they received the promised gift of the Holy Spirit and spoke in tongues.

The Apostle Paul said, "You were sealed with the *Holy Spirit of promise!*" This phrase has a specific meaning that can be noted in the following passages:

- Luke 24:49   I send the promise of my Father
- Acts 1:4   Wait for the promise of the Father
- Acts 2:33   receive the promise of the Holy Spirit
- Acts 2:39   this promise is to you and your children
- Ephesians 1:13   sealed with the Holy Spirit of promise

In every one of these scriptures, the promise refers to the baptism of the Holy Spirit as the disciples received it on the Day of Pentecost. This does not happen when a person receives Christ as Savior, but *after* the person believes. The Holy Spirit is the Spirit of truth, "whom the world [unconverted] cannot receive, because it neither sees Him nor knows Him; but you know Him, for He dwells with you and *will be in you*" (John 14:17). Again, there is a difference in dimension—*with* you and *in* you!

If the disciples had been "sealed with the Holy Spirit of promise" when they accepted Jesus as Lord, there would have been no need for them to wait for the "promise of the Father" in Jerusalem as Jesus instructed. If the disciples of Samaria had been sealed with the Holy Spirit of promise when they were saved in that great revival of salvation, healing, and deliverance, then an additional experience would have been superfluous. But...

> when the apostles who were at Jerusalem heard that Samaria had received the word of God, they sent Peter and John to them, who, when they had come down, prayed for them that they might receive the Holy Spirit. *For as yet He had fallen upon none of them.*
>
> Acts 8:14–16 (*emphasis mine*)

The seal is an *earnest* of our inheritance until the time of redemption. In other words, it is like a down payment, earnest money, until the time we receive in full all that is coming to us. The baptism of the Holy Spirit is like an engagement ring. Our heavenly bridegroom is saying, *This is just a little token of all that is yours because you belong to me!*

There's a lot waiting for us at the end of our journey with the King of kings. But as we travel, we rejoice because life in the Spirit is really a *Great* Adventure!

Expression: A New Language

As the Nineteenth Century was drawing to a close, God began to cause hungry hearts to seek a deeper walk with God. Some said there was a "baptism of fire" taught in the Bible that believers should receive. Others called for a "third blessing" (sanctification being the second). Still others preached about an infilling or baptism of the Holy Spirit.

In Kansas City in the year 1900, Charles Parham had a small Bible School. On one occasion, he gave his students a specific assignment about the Holy Spirit. They were to read the accounts in the Book of Acts where people were "filled with" or "received" the Holy Spirit and then decide how other people knew when someone received this experience. What was the evidence of having been "baptized" in the Holy Spirit? They found five specific incidents of this experience in the Book of Acts:

1. Acts 2:4
2. Acts 8:17
3. Acts 9:17, 18
4. Acts 10:44–46
5. Acts 19:6

1. Day of Pentecost
2. Philip in Samaria
3. Ananias/ Saul
4. Home of Cornelius
5. Ephesus

1. They were "filled with the Holy Spirit, and began to speak with other tongues."

2. They received the Holy Spirit.

3. The Lord…sent me, that you might receive your sight and be filled with the Holy Spirit.

4. They heard them speak with tongues and magnify God.

5. The Holy Spirit came upon them, and they spoke with tongues and prophesied.

Those students concluded that the biblical evidence of receiving the baptism of the Holy Spirit was speaking in tongues. They came to this decision because of what they found in the Book of Acts where people were filled with the Spirit on these five different occasions. In three of the five events, it states definitely that they spoke with tongues. In the one where Saul (Paul) received the Holy Spirit, it does not definitely state in the Acts account that he spoke with tongues. We are not in doubt, however, as to the manifestation of tongues in his life, because he himself said in 1 Corinthians 14:18, "I thank my God I speak with tongues more than you all."

Is there evidence that the people who received the Holy Spirit in Samaria also spoke in tongues? My answer is yes.

Simon saw something visible happen when these believers received this experience and offered Peter and John money, saying, "Give me this power also, that anyone on whom I lay hands may receive the Holy Spirit" (Acts 8:19). What did Simon see? God had already moved in a mighty revival under the preaching of Philip. They had seen miracles, healings, and deliverance from evil spirits and there was great joy in the city (Acts 8:6–8). But "as yet He [the Holy Spirit] had fallen upon none of them" (Acts 8:16). It is only logical to conclude that Simon saw the people begin to speak in tongues just as the Bible says they spoke on the other occasions.

It is indicated in Acts 10:44–46 that the speaking in tongues was what identified the receiving of the Holy Spirit. "The gift of the Holy Spirit had been poured out on the Gentiles also. For *they heard them speak with tongues and magnify God*...Can anyone forbid water, that these should not be baptized *who have received the Holy Spirit just as we have?*" (*Emphasis mine.*)

The Bible School students read again Acts 2:38–39 the words Peter spoke on the Day of Pentecost. "You shall receive the gift of the Holy Spirit. For the promise is to you and to your children, and to all who are afar off, as many as the Lord our God shall call." That the promise was for them and succeeding generations was confirmed again by Peter's quoting of Joel's prophecy, "And it shall come to pass in the last days, says God, that I will pour out of My Spirit on all flesh; Your sons and your daughters shall prophesy" (Acts 2:17). The director of the school, Charles Parham, had not received nor seen anyone receive a baptism of the Holy

Spirit. Neither had any of the students had any such experience. But just as the Twentieth Century was being ushered in, one member of the group, Agnes Ozman, became the first historically recorded person in this century to receive this baptism of the Holy Spirit and to speak with new tongues.

Some people are not interested in receiving this experience because they simply do not see any need for the tongues that go along with it. As far as they are concerned, tongues have no use in the on-going work of the kingdom. So it is necessary to consider what the benefits of tongues are.

Tongues are evidence that you have received the baptism of the Holy Spirit.

Jesus informed us that the Holy Spirit would speak when He came. The Holy Spirit "will not speak on His own authority, but whatever He hears *He will speak;* and He will tell you things to come" (John 16:13, *Emphasis mine*). Jesus also said that when the Holy Spirit is come, "he shall testify of me" (John 15:26). No person can testify without speaking! Jesus had told them to expect tongues. "And these signs shall follow those who believe: In My name...they will speak with new tongues" (Mark 16:17). On the Day of Pentecost, the Holy Spirit spoke through the believers just as Jesus said He would. "They were all filled with the Holy Spirit and began to speak with other tongues, as the Spirit gave them utterance" (Acts 2:4).

Speaking in other tongues is a continuing evidence.

When the Holy Spirit speaks through me in tongues,
I know He is saying, "I'm still here!" Although I accept
tongues as the evidence of the presence of the Holy Spirit,
I also understand that this is not the only evidence. Jesus
said, "You shall receive *power*," and He also said, "You shall
be witnesses."

Prophetic words may follow immediately after a person receives the initial evidence of tongues, but they do not constitute a continuing biblical pattern.

Speaking in tongues is the biblical pattern for receiving the
baptism of the Spirit, but the gift of prophecy may also be
present. You must not feel that you were not filled with the
Spirit, however, if after speaking in tongues you did not also
prophecy. In Ephesus when they received the gift of the
Holy Spirit, they both "spoke with tongues *and prophesied*"
(Acts 19:6). Nothing is said, however, about any accompanying prophetic words on the Day of Pentecost by those
who were filled (Acts 2:4). In the home of Cornelius where
the Spirit was poured out, there is no mention of the gift of
prophecy. It simply says that "they heard them speak with
tongues and magnify God" (Acts 10:44, 45). The gift of
the Holy Spirit is a gateway for the manifestation of other
gifts of the Spirit and the most common list is found in 1
Corinthians 12:7–11.

Devotional tongues are important in the life of the believer in private and in public.

Devotional tongues edify the believer in private. The Holy Spirit is very much a part of the devotional life, and the Spirit will manifest Himself in the secret place of our worship. Paul sang in the Spirit and prayed in the Spirit. This truly edifies and lifts us up.

The Holy Spirit also edifies believers in public service. Sometimes an entire congregation may worship before the Lord in tongues of praise and song. Is this biblical? Yes! On the Day of Pentecost, they were *all* filled with the Spirit and began to speak with other tongues together. This was not only the order on the Day of Pentecost, but also in Cornelius' house and in Ephesus. Simultaneous praise in the native tongue or in unknown tongues has always been a part of Pentecostal worship. Interpretation is necessary when a *message* is given in tongues but not for devotional praise.

Tongues are your heavenly language.

When you don't know how to pray, let the Spirit take over. He will often reveal to you the need you are asking Him about and let you know how to pray with understanding. This is a valuable asset to you in the ministry of intercession.

> Likewise, the Spirit also helps in our weaknesses. For we do not know what we should pray for as we ought, but the Spirit Himself makes intercession for us with groanings which cannot be uttered. Now He

who searches the hearts knows what the mind of the Spirit is, because He makes intercession for the saints according to the will of God.

Romans 8:26, 27

Devotional tongues should be a continuous flow.

Some might say, "I spoke with tongues years ago when I received the baptism of the Spirit, but not any more." Jesus said,

He who believes in Me, as the Scripture has said, out of his heart will flow rivers of living water. But this He spoke concerning the Spirit, whom those believing in Him would receive; for the Holy Spirit was not yet given, because Jesus was not yet glorified.

John 7:38, 39

What stopped the river that was supposed to flow out of your innermost being? The Holy Spirit can and should be continually flowing to guide and direct you in all truth. The Spirit will "show you things to come" (John 16:13). He will call you, guide you, and reveal to you His will for the future.

There is a difference between the "Gift of the Holy Spirit" and the "Gift of Tongues."

The Gift of the Holy Spirit
The 120 received the "gift of the Holy Spirit" in the Upper Room on the day of Pentecost, and Peter told the people in

the street, "Repent, and be baptized…and you shall receive the gift of the Holy Spirit." This gift was accompanied by the speaking in tongues as evidence of its reception, and opened the door for other manifestations to follow. When you were baptized in the Spirit, you received the gift of the Holy Spirit that was promised to all who would believe and accept (Acts 2:38, 39), and you spoke in tongues as evidence of that reception. Tongues came as evidence of the presence of the Holy Spirit in your life, and if you continue to speak with tongues, you will know that the Holy Spirit is still there.

The Gift of Tongues

Spiritual tongues manifest themselves in three different ways—as the initial evidence of receiving the baptism of the Holy Spirit, as devotional tongues, and as the gift of tongues. This third manifestation of tongues is a *message* in tongues that must be interpreted in order that the church may be edified. The body of believers will not know the meaning of the message unless it is interpreted. In 1 Corinthians 12:7–11, the Apostle Paul gives a list of manifestations of the Spirit, translated as gifts in the King James Version. Among these are the three vocal gifts: prophecy, tongues, and interpretation of tongues. Prophecy is a message in the native tongue and is for edification, exhortation, and comfort; it may also tell of "things to come" (1 Corinthians 14:3, John 16:13). Tongues accompanied by interpretation equal prophecy; both edify the congregation and the believer. Both are subject to the same guidelines of conduct.

Guidelines for the gift of tongues

Guidelines for the gift of tongues operate on a different set of rules than those of devotional tongues or tongues as evidence. When someone has the floor and gives a message in tongues, the person who gives the message or another should interpret. If a person gives messages and no one interprets them, there are two things for that person to keep in mind:

1. He should pray to be able to interpret. In 1 Corinthians 14:13, the Apostle Paul makes this very clear. "Therefore let him who speaks in a tongue pray that he may interpret." One person may give a message and another interprets, or the person giving the message may interpret.

2. If no one interprets, he should keep silent. "But if there is no interpreter, let him keep silent in church, and let him speak to himself and to God (1 Corinthians 14:28). He may be confusing something that God is saying to him personally with a message for the congregation.

Messages are not to be given simultaneously, but one after the other.

Each message is to be given in turn, and each is to be interpreted. "If anyone speaks in a tongue, let there be two or at the most three, each in turn, and let one interpret" (1 Corinthians 14:27). If someone has a message, others are to keep silent. "If anything is revealed to another who sits by, let the first keep silent" (1 Corinthians 14:30). This includes music, singing, and others who may be vocally worshipping the Lord. Only then can the congregation hear what the Spirit is saying.

Those who give messages (by prophecy or by tongues and interpretation) are subject to the pastor or leader of the congregation (1 Corinthians 14:32, 33).

It is the pastor's responsibility to see that all is done decently and in order for the edification of the church. Everyone is to understand that if there is necessary correction, it is being done on the authority of God's Word.

Love is the sign of the presence of the Holy Spirit.

The reality of the presence of the Holy Spirit in the church is evident when believers show love to one another. God is love; even when a minister has to correct, reprove, or rebuke, it must be done in love. If a prophecy or message in tongues and interpretation is an exhortation or correction but is not administered in love, it will have a negative value. The Apostle Paul said, "Though I speak with the tongues of men and of angels, but have not love, I have become sounding brass or a clanging cymbal" (1 Corinthians 13:1). Jesus actually made love the badge of discipleship when He said, "By this all will know that you are My disciples, if you have love for one another" (John 13:35).

Forbid not to speak with tongues.

Many pastors, teachers, and other leaders use God's Word to teach against what the Lord has so graciously made available to us. These ministers *do forbid to speak in tongues* in their congregations. In 1 Corinthians 12 and 14, Paul gives instructions about the manifestation of the gifts of the Holy Spirit. Most people would be glad to have the word of wisdom, word of knowledge, faith, healings, working of miracles, and discerning of spirits; the problem comes with this evidence of the tongues. The Apostle deals with these manifestations in the entirety of these two chapters, and gives guidelines about them:

- They are to operate for the edifying of the church.

- They are to function "decently and in order."

- They are to be administered in love.

- "Messages" in tongues should be interpreted for the edifying of the body of believers.

- Tongues are not to be forbidden (1 Corinthians 14:39).

If we are forbidden to speak in tongues, why should these guidelines on the manifestation of these gifts even be in the Bible? The Apostle Paul is clearly telling us that these manifestations are in the church and that they should function. He also explains *how* they are to function. People are not to preach or counsel in a tongue others don't understand. The church must be edified, so the Apostle tells us that it is better to have the manifestation of prophecy, unless a message in tongues is interpreted. Prophecy edifies, but as previously mentioned, tongues plus interpretation also edifies (1 Corinthians 14:12, 13). So in the preaching/ teaching ministry, Paul says he would rather speak five words the people understand than ten thousand in another language.

Was the Apostle Paul against speaking in tongues? Certainly not. He says, "I speak in tongues more than you all" (1 Corinthians 14:18), "do not forbid to speak in tongues" (1 Corinthians 14:39), and beside all this he affirms, "I will pray with the spirit, and I will also pray with the understanding. I will sing with the spirit, and I will also sing with the understanding" (1 Corinthians 14:15). He would continue to be blessed as he ministered before the Lord in the move of the spiritual gifts.

Some people pick out the following scripture and tell us that tongues have ceased.

> "But whether there are prophecies, they will fail; *whether there are tongues, they will cease;* whether there is knowledge, it will vanish away. For we know in part and we prophecy in part. But when that which is perfect has come, then that which is in part will be done away."

> 1 Corinthians 13:8–10 (*emphasis mine*)

People who believe that tongues have already ceased tell us that it is because that which is perfect has come, meaning that we now have the full canon of the Bible. Yet, the Bible is full of many prophecies yet to be fulfilled. Will those prophecies fail since we now have the Bible? No! "Till heaven and earth pass away, one jot or one title will by no means pass from the law till all is fulfilled" (Matthew 5:18). Has knowledge vanished away? Indeed not! In fact, we are living in a day of the explosion of knowledge. How wonderful it would be if there were an explosion of the knowledge of God! Paul exhorts us in Colossians 1: 9 saying, we "do not cease to pray for you, and to ask that you may be filled with *the knowledge* of His will in all wisdom and spiritual understanding." And in Ephesians 1:17–18, he prays that God may give "the spirit of wisdom and revelation in *the knowledge* of Him, the eyes of your understanding being enlightened." I don't think Paul was expecting knowledge to cease until that time when, in our glorified bodies, we would see our Lord face to face and know truly that "that which is perfect" has come.

In fact, "that which is perfect" refers to the glorified body, when all the saints are "changed—in a moment, in the twinkling of an eye, at the last trumpet. For the trumpet will sound, and the dead will be raised incorruptible, and we shall be changed" (1 Corinthians 15:51, 52). When that happens there will be no more need of prophecy, messages in tongues, or interpretation of tongues.

These were lessons I came to understand over a period of time as I learned to swim in the waters of the Spirit. I'm a bit embarrassed about it, but I can't swim in natural waters. I might be able to float, however, while you count to ten. But one day the Lord invited me to move on out into the deep of spiritual waters, and I learned the joy of swimming in the waters of the Spirit. I am well aware that there are many areas into which I have yet to move, and the Lord always beacons me on to higher heights and in to deeper dimensions in Him. In the Spirit there is light, wisdom, revelation, and understanding.

Until we see Christ face to face, there will always be new battles to fight, fierce enemies to overcome, and greater victories to proclaim. But, let's move on! Life's Great Adventure is really one of joy and excitement as we journey with the King of all kings!

Preparation

I graduated from the Muskogee, Oklahoma, Central High School the year Daddy took the pastorate of our congregation there. I had become a sort of Girl Friday for him, and I consider that ministry a part of my training in Practical Theology. I had taught a Sunday school class since I was a young teenager and continued to serve in that capacity as well as in the youth and worship ministries. Besides playing the piano or accordion in the church services, I typed most of Daddy's sermon outlines. This was important for two reasons: first, Daddy had a hard time reading his own script once it got cold; and second, his hunt and peck system on the little portable typewriter was slow-going. Daddy was good at homiletical arrangement, so this service to him would serve me later on.

My stepsister Wanda and I had been in the same class at school since the third grade, so we also got to graduate together. I had lacked just a couple of high school credits, so after class, I was able to work part-time at the S. H. Kress store. During that time they promoted me up from the hosiery department to counting money in the office, and that promotion won me a trophy on the day I graduated.

Then I decided to apply for work with Southwestern Bell Telephone Company since their beginning pay was about 30% more than I was earning at Kress. Meanwhile, there were some issues I had to face. I knew I would start at the bottom of their work totem pole, and I already knew the rules. Would I be willing to sacrifice my work for the Lord in order to adapt to the shift work, night hours, and the Sundays that would be involved in making the change? The shift work and evening hours would mean that I would not be able to regularly attend revivals, special events, or midweek services. I couldn't continue to direct the youth group. Sunday work meant that I would have to miss either the morning or evening service most Sundays. That would mean giving up teaching in the Sunday school. How important were these things to me?

My only reason for changing jobs was the extra money that I would earn. If I had that extra money in my hand, what could I possibly buy that would satisfy me more than the work I did in service to the Lord? I tried to weigh the factors in the balance of eternal values, and I decided that the new job just wouldn't be worth the extra money. If I gained the world and grew cold in my spirit, was it worth it? If I caused another youth, who might be watching me, to make a wrong decision, was I willing to bear the consequences? I was well aware that many people had to work those hours and days, but *I* didn't have to.

They called me from the company. "Miss North, you have been selected to come in for an interview. I would like to set a time that will be convenient for you."

I answered without hesitation. "I'm very sorry if I have inconvenienced you, but there are some aspects of the job that won't fit in with other things I'm doing. Thank you very much for considering me as a future employee, but I must withdraw my application." I took a deep breath and praised the Lord that He had given me the courage to make the right decision.

There was no college in Muskogee for me, so I just continued on with S. H. Kress and my work at the church. I knew Daddy depended on me a lot—but what were my own goals in life? It was during this time that Dr. R. O. Corvin, the president of our church's school in Oklahoma City, Southwestern Bible College (now Southwestern Christian University), brought a group of young people to visit the church. They were promoting the college and recruiting students. I saw young men and young women with purpose written on their faces. They were preparing for the future, and something clicked. I knew my "on-the job-training" with Daddy had been a valuable part of my preparation, but the time had come to take another step forward. After the service, those students surrounded me and told me they would really like to see me attend Southwestern. Their welcome sounded warm, and I enrolled as a student for the next semester, which would begin just after the New Year.

Evelyn (my sister) and I had both worked at the Ana Maude Cafeteria in Oklahoma City when we had lived there, and although three years had passed, I telephoned the personnel supervisor. I explained that I would be attending college and would have to pay for my own expenses. Would there be a place in the cafeteria for me to work? Without hesitation she said, "Come on in. I'll have a place for you, and you can begin work when you get here." This, indeed, was when I began to understand the importance of moving in God's timing. The doors opened to me might not always be the ones I should enter, and the doors that closed were messages from God. A door would open, and the Lord Himself would give me that spiritual nudge I needed, and I would hear him say, "This is the way—walk in it."

Dormitory life was a good experience for me. I had early classes with lots of homework, but after chapel I was free to go to my job. I studied as I stood at the bus stop in the icy January wind that swept down Northwest Tenth Street. The bus was often full, but I usually had a paper in my hand, memorizing the cities of refuge or some other such detail that was sure to appear on the next test. I worked until 8:00 p.m., and it was usually about 9:00 p.m. by the time I got back to the dorm.

I learned to discipline myself and program my time. I got up early to study and prepare for my classes, and I studied going to and from work. Some times I only got in on the tail end of the social activities, but I was as involved as this full-schedule allowed me to be. The high light of that semester was to go on the Southwestern College Choir Tour and to sing in the churches on the way to the General Conference in Jacksonville, Florida. It was my first time to cross the Mississippi—and my first time to eat grits!

What does *preparing for the future* mean? Well, it means teaching baby lips to pray and praise the Lord. It means the socializing and interaction of children as they learn that pulling other children's hair and biting are unacceptable. It means loving people, even if they're really unlovely. It means obeying and honoring parents when the only reason seems to be "because I told you so." There's even reason behind that, because we also have to learn to obey and honor God when we don't understand the circumstances that come our way. Being prepared means taking disappointments in our stride, like the time Daddy comforted me when somebody else bought the accordion I had intended to buy. I just had to believe Daddy when he said that God had something better for me—and He did.

But for me, being prepared also meant being at Southwestern at this point in time. I didn't go to prepare for a pulpit ministry. I had no call to preach, pastor, or be a missionary. But I was studying the Bible as never before, as well as other subjects vital to Christian service. I really couldn't see beyond the first two years at Southwestern, because the last two were primarily subjects for ministerial preparation.

In the fall semester, I was one of those students who got to visit churches to promote the college and recruit students. Dr. Corvin liked for us to introduce ourselves—give our names and tell where we were from. Sometimes after I introduced myself, he would say, "Miss North isn't called to preach. I think she's just called to be a preacher's wife!" (Yes, it always drew a good laugh!)

As I looked toward the future, I could only feel that being a preacher's wife was my destiny. But *where* was the preacher? He didn't have to be that tall, dark, and handsome guy you read about in romantic novels (I myself didn't fall into that romantic category), but he had to be…good looking. A person who knew how to dress and always looked nice; one I could be proud to walk beside. But above every-thing else, he had to be a good preacher! After all, I had only had one pastor in my lifetime; I had always enjoyed sitting under Daddy's ministry and hearing him preach. I couldn't imagine the torture of sitting under the preaching—year after year—of someone who really had no anointing to preach! I think it was because Daddy was my hero that I was willing to bear all the blessings and possible ills that would come with being a preacher's wife!

I didn't have a lot of free time. It was class, work, the dorm, study, and more work. But one of my three roommates called my attention to a young man who had transferred to Southwestern from Emmanuel College in Georgia for the last two years of his ministerial study. His name interested me—Russel West. My mother's maiden name was Russell, and then his last name was a direction!

The roommate who called my attention to Russel also called his attention to me, and he invited me to the first college social in the autumn. I didn't know it, of course, but he had a long list of qualifications for the girl who would be his future wife.

You know, of course, that Jesus our Lord is looking for a bride—a people who will choose to love and serve Him, not just for what He gives them, but for who He is. And He has qualifications for *His* bride.

> Christ loved the church and gave Himself for her, that He might sanctify and cleanse her with the washing of water by the word, that He might pres-ent her to Himself a glorious church, not having spot

or wrinkle or any such thing, but that she should be
holy and without blemish.

Ephesians 5:25–27

The bride our Lord is seeking is also occupied in His
kingdom activities. We have been saved to follow in His
footsteps and to fulfill His purposes in the world. His words
to His first disciples were, "Follow me and I'll make you
fishers of men." To all of us He has said, "Go and tell others." Saul of Tarsus met Christ on the road to Damascus;
once converted, his words were, "What do you want me
to do?" (Acts 9:6), and He immediately began to work for
the Lord. A love affair is going on between Christ and His
chosen people. His Helper, the Holy Spirit, seeks out those
who will listen, and He is constantly reminding them to be
what Jesus wants in His holy bride. He tells us that many
are called, but few are chosen. (If you're really serious about
this, you can find all the qualifications written down quite
clearly in the book He has left us. It is called the Holy
Bible.) I challenge you to become one of the Lord's chosen
ones!

Under the circumstances, Southwestern (with its no-
touch rules for the opposite sex at that time) perhaps was
not the easiest place to get acquainted. But guess what?
There are places in the world where it is far from easy to
get acquainted with Jesus. In fact some people are impris-
oned, tortured, and killed because they have pledged their
allegiance to the Lordship of Christ. But although some
pay the ultimate price to follow the Lord, the Holy Spirit
will always be on the lookout for you! There is no prison

that can shut *Him* out! And He will see that you really get acquainted with the King of kings!

Russel and I began to watch out for each other and sit together in chapel. I learned that he was a member of the Western North Carolina Conference and had pastored a small congregation before coming to Southwestern. He could not ignore his divine call to preach, but the pastors in Oklahoma didn't know him and naturally didn't invite him into their pulpits. After all, Southwestern was inhabited by preachers and would-be preachers. So Russel asked the Lord to give him a place to preach. He found it by getting permission from municipal authorities to preach on a street corner in downtown Oklahoma City. His listeners lived on the fringes of society, but his faithfulness opened other doors and a broader ministry for him. He and other Southwestern students also carried on a prison ministry.

When the pastors heard about this young man from the East who had come West and found out that his passion for the lost urged him to a pulpit on the edge of Oklahoma City's red-light district, they began to invite him into their churches for youth services and weekend revivals. Russel didn't have to work on a secular job while he was at school, so he had more time to accept these invitations.

I asked him about his plans for the Thanksgiving holiday, and it seems he was waiting for me to invite him to spend it with my family in Muskogee! Holidays were always special in the parsonage with the North family. All of us were together—Mom and Dad, sisters, brothers, and brothers-in-law. They made Russel feel at home and handed him their car keys. It was nice to be free from college restrictions and show Russel what Muskogee looked like. Meanwhile, the dining room table piled with the abundance of food. Nothing smelled quite like Mom's hot yeast rolls, and the house was also full of other delicious odors. Only one thing kept me on edge. I never knew what Gerald and Charles, my younger brothers, would come up with. They were masters at hiding in unusual places, hearing things not meant for their ears, and pulling jokes. The weekend, however, got by without any disaster from that area—a good angel must have been helping me out!

Daddy invited Russel to preach for him on Sunday, and I heard him preach for the first time. People were blessed and responded. It was very evident that a special anointing of the Holy Spirit rested on him and his ministry. The Muskogee people were so very special, and after church many of them slipped by me and whispered in my ear, "He's the one! Don't let him get away!"

The weeks between Thanksgiving and Christmas were courtship time, and we came to know and appreciate one another. Without my realizing it, Russel was checking off his qualification list…one of those things being that the girl he married must be able to play the piano, because he didn't. To him nothing would be sadder than a church without music, praise, and worship. Well, I do play the piano, the accordion, and other keyboard instruments, but I wasn't aware that I was fulfilling a requirement! He also believed that inner holiness was reflected on the outside, and it seems I pleased him on that score.

I invited Russel to Muskogee again for Christmas, and it was during those days that he told me he loved me and asked me to be his wife. I told him he would have to talk to my parents—and he did! I know Daddy was happy. If none of his children were going to be preachers, at least he would have one for a son-in-law.

Well, Dr. Corvin came up with another joke. "Mr. *West* came from the *East* (in fact from *North* Carolina heeding the advice of Horace Greeley, the newspaperman, 'Go *West*, young man, go *West*,') and when he got to *Southwestern* College, he met a young lady named Miss *North!*" His joke was appreciated then and has survived the decades. Even now people I hardly know say to me, "Oh, yes…I remember that joke about West from the East meeting North!

Those pre-nuptial days and weeks were important. Time for new plans had to be squeezed in without neglecting work and studies. The invitations had to be sent out, my sister Gertrude was making my dress, Mom was baking the cake, and there was the wedding party to form. It was fun, it was exciting, and at times it was exhausting! And even with the final exams of the semester to study for, most of my thoughts were on that big evening when we would exchange our vows and begin a new life together.

The bride of Christ, those very special ones the Lord is wooing for His own, are singing their commitment. "I have decided to follow Jesus, I won't turn back; I won't turn back—Take this whole world, but give me Jesus. I won't turn back!" John, on the Isle of Patmos, by revelation looked into the future and saw the bride of Christ in all the resplendent glory of her wedding finery. All heaven will rejoice when that day of all days becomes a reality.

And I heard, as it were, the voice of a great multitude, as the sound of many waters and as the sound of mighty thunderings, saying, "Alleluia! For the Lord God Omnipotent reigns! Let us be glad and rejoice and give Him glory, for the marriage of the Lamb has come, and His wife has made herself ready." And to her it was granted to be arrayed in fine linen, clean and bright, for the fine linen is the righteous acts of the saints.

Revelation 19:6–8

One thing that has always impressed me about this scripture is that we ourselves are preparing our wedding clothes with what we do for the Lord. The fine linen, clean and bright, is woven out of the "righteous acts of the saints." Every day, with the words I speak for Christ, with the testimonies I share, with any act of kindness, etc., I myself am weaving the cloth out of which my wedding garment will be made.

The wedding day of our Lord is anticipated with great expectancy. The invitations have been sent out, all preparations have been made, and everything is there—except the date. We don't know the day, the hour, or the time, so it means that we live in anticipation of His return for us. We do not doubt His coming, because just as everything concerning his first coming was fulfilled, we are just as sure that everything for His future return will take place exactly as it has been foretold.

Well, the time and place were announced for our wedding. Daddy would marry us in the Muskogee church on May 26, 1950. Just as soon as classes were over at Southwestern, our marriage would take place. Since Muskogee was about three hours east of Oklahoma City, many of those in the wedding party would be well on their return home from college. They were just stopping over to be with us as we celebrated the exchanging of our vows. This was the day we had waited for. All the preparations had been made. I was ready, and Russel was standing somewhere nearby.

Many people have met the Lord and have become acquainted with Him through His Word. They know the significance of his death, burial, and resurrection. They may even call Him "Lord," and work for the extension of His Kingdom here on earth. Perhaps they are faithful members of a Bible-believing church, but they have never really been in love with Jesus. They haven't learned the joy of meeting Him in the secret place of the Most High and of sitting at His feet.

Those who love the Lord have watched for His return since that day the disciples saw Him disappear into the heavens and heard the angels say, "Men of Galilee, why do you stand gazing up into heaven? This same Jesus, who was taken up from you into heaven, will so come in like manner as you saw Him go into heaven" (Acts 1:11). They looked for Him as they traversed the deserts and as they sailed the high seas. Their eyes swept the horizons as they topped the hills and mountains. *Maranatha!* (*Our Lord is coming!*), they greeted other Christians who had stamped somewhere on their belongings the crude sign of a fish.

> *Oh, He's coming back, for He said He would,* (Daddy would sing)
> *Yes, He's coming back again.*

With the sound of a trumpet and the voice of an archangel,
He's coming back to earth again!

I have looked for Him all my life and have endeavored to be prepared for His return, because I understand that the church is living in its "day of preparation." I can see signs that point to the end-times in areas of the *prophetic,* the *scientific,* and the *spiritual* as well as the *missionary* arenas of our modern world. And then, of course, probably the most outstanding sign of all is the return of the Jews to their homeland and the rebirth of Israel as a nation.

I must say that none of these have *had* to take place before the rapture of the saints. The church has never been told to wait until certain things happen for that great event to take place—but to always be prepared for the Lord's return. We have been told to live in readiness, to watch, and to wait, because we do not know when Jesus will come for us.

To what do these signs point then? They point to things that must take place before Christ returns to set up His Kingdom. Between the rapture and the Lord's return to defeat His enemies at Armageddon and the setting up of His Kingdom, there will be seven years of tribulation. The Antichrist will appear on the world's stage of action and make a seven-year covenant of peace. He will convince the nations that he has the answer to the ills of this planet and become a world dictator during the last three-and-one-half years of the Tribulation.

God's Word assures us that the saints will be caught away before the wrath of God is poured out upon the kingdom of Antichrist and this apostate world. Jesus warned us,

"Watch therefore, and pray always that you may be counted worthy to escape all these things that will come to pass, and to stand before the Son of Man" (Luke 21:36). Isaiah also writes of a time of great distress before which God's people will be hidden away. In so doing, He describes the rapture and the beginning of the Tribulation Period.

> Come, my people, enter your chambers, and shut your doors behind you; Hide yourself, as it were, for a little moment, until the indignation is past. For behold, the Lord comes out of His place to punish the inhabitants of the earth for their iniquity.
>
> Isaiah 26:20, 21

Scientific Signs:

Daddy was a great student of the prophetic word, and he was interested in how world-news fit in with end-time events. He could see modern inventions in their prophetic light and observed that God's Word was being fulfilled during our own time. He also believed that we were living in the time of God's "preparation."

- The automobile was foretold about in God's Word.

> The chariots come with flaming torches in the day of his preparation. And the spears are brandished. The chariots rage in the streets, They jostle one another in the broad roads; They seem like torches, they run like lightning.
>
> Nahum 2:3, 4

- Airplanes were seen in a prophecy that was put into action and helped win Israel's Seven-Day War. "Like birds flying about, so will the Lord of hosts defend Jerusalem. Defending, He will also deliver it; passing over, He will preserve it" (Isaiah 31:5).

- Antichrist is the next great political world dictator, and the stage for his appearance is already being set to usher in his kingdom. His reign will be Satan's last effort to win the world, and Scripture graphically describes him. He is…

> the man of sin…revealed [and] the son of perdition, who opposes and exalts himself above all that is called God or that is worshiped, so that he sits as God in the temple of God, showing himself that he is God.
>
> 2 Thessalonians 2:3, 4

- He will dominate nations, control individuals, and destroy all those who oppose him. His mark will be a worldwide ID, and everyone will be expected to receive it. It is the number of his name—666. An economic numbering system is already in place. Even newborn babies in the U.S. are now given Social Security numbers, and the use of information chips to identify people is also being implemented.

> He causes all, both small and great, rich and poor, free and slave, to receive a mark on their right hand or on their foreheads, and that no one may buy or sell except one who has the mark of the beast, or the

number of his name. Here is wisdom. Let him who has understanding calculate the number of the beast, for it is the number of a man. His number is 666.

Revelation 13:16–18

- The mark of the Antichrist constitutes eternal damnation.

If anyone worships the beast and his image, and receives his mark on his forehead or on his hand, he himself shall also drink of the wine of the wrath of God, which is poured out full strength into the cup of his indignation. He shall be tormented with fire and brimstone in the presence of the holy angels and in the presence of the Lamb. And the smoke of their torment ascends forever and ever; and they have no rest day or night…

Revelation 14:9–11

- Satellite television makes it possible for worldwide events to be *seen* simultaneously. Think of this scripture when the two witnesses during the Tribulation are killed by the Antichrist:

Then *those from the peoples, tribes, tongues, and nations will see* their dead bodies three-and-a-half days, and not allow their dead bodies to be put into graves. And those who dwell on the earth will rejoice over them, make merry, and send gifts to one another, because these two prophets tormented those who dwell on the earth.

Revelation 11:9–11 (*Emphasis mine*)

- Machines and images that speak. "Thank you for your business," some machines now say after a transaction.

> He was granted to give breath to the image of the beast, that the image of the beast would both speak and cause as many as would not worship the image of the beast to be killed.
>
> Revelation 13:15

Spiritual Signs

A worldwide Pentecostal revival began at the beginning of the Twentieth Century and was welcomed as a revival to prepare God's people for an end-time harvest before the Lord's return. Joel prophesied of this revival, and Peter quoted his words on the Day of Pentecost.

> But this is what was spoken by the prophet Joel: And it shall come to pass in the last days, says God, That I will pour out of my Spirit on all flesh; Your sons and your daughters shall prophesy, Your young men shall see visions, Your old men shall dream dreams. And on My menservants and on My maidservants I will pour out My Spirit in those days; and they shall prophesy.
>
> Acts 2:16–18

Isaiah also tells us about this outpouring. "And I will pour water on him who is thirsty, and floods on the dry ground; I will pour My Spirit on your descendants, and My blessing on your offspring" (Isaiah 44:3, 4).

Jesus taught about this endowment of power and called it the "promise of the Father." This spiritual equipment from God was what His people needed to fulfill the task He had given them to go into all the world with the Gospel. The Early Church ministered under this anointing, and the Book of Acts is full of events directed, motivated, and carried out in the power of the Holy Spirit. The Apostle Paul dedicated prime space in his first epistle to the Corinthians about the ministry of the Spirit, and there is no doubt that the fire of the Holy Spirit burned in the hearts of the people of the Apostolic Church. With the passing of time, however, the Church grew cold. Spiritual matters were left to the clergy; there was limited access to God's written Word, and the gifts of the Spirit were shelved.

God began a spiritual renewal, however, with the Reformation that started under Martin Luther. The Bible was translated into the language of the people, the doctrine of salvation by faith was brought back into focus, and later John Wesley appeared to remind the church that without holiness no one would see the Lord. It was the Pentecostal revival, however, that came as the new century was ushered in that placed a special emphasis on the Second Coming of the Lord. Spirit-filled preachers declared that this was the outpouring of the "last days" about which Joel prophesied; this was the "latter rain" to mature the fields for an end-time revival. This was what James told us we must wait for.

> Therefore be patient, brethren, until the coming of the Lord. See how the farmer waits for the precious fruit of the earth, waiting patiently for it until it

receives the early and latter rain. You also be patient. Establish your hearts, for the coming of the Lord is at hand.

James 5:7, 8

People also related the words of Jesus found in Acts 1:8 to those found in Matthew 24:14. Jesus said they would receive power to witness in the entire world: "But you shall receive power when the Holy Spirit has come upon you; and you shall be witnesses to Me in Jerusalem, and in all Judea, and Samaria, and to the end of the earth" (Acts 1:8). Jesus also said that the gospel would be preached in the whole world before the end-time. "And this gospel of the kingdom will be preached in all the world as a witness to all the nations, and then the end will come." (Matthew 24:14).

It is understood why, then, that the Pentecostal out-pouring spawned a new movement of world missions. The Holy Spirit called dedicated people to the ends of the earth. Missionaries went to Asia, Africa, China, Latin America and the islands of the sea. There is no continent that has been left untouched by the Gospel message carried by Spirit-filled ministers.

The Sign of Israel

There is no sign, however, that speaks to us of the Lord's return more forcefully than the rebirth of Israel as a nation. God had warned Israel that if she rejected Him, she would be scattered and that "Jerusalem would be trodden down." Jeremiah 31:10 tells us that they would be scattered, but that they would be brought back again. "He who scattered Israel will gather him, and keep him as a shepherd does his flock."

On November 29, 1947, the United Nations General Assembly agreed to divide Palestine into Arab and Jewish states and to put Jerusalem under international control. Israel officially became a Jewish state on May 14, 1948, and the new nation raised her flag bearing the Star of David—a nation born in a day. The next day, however, a coalition of Arab armies from Egypt, Syria, Lebanon, Iraq, and Jordan combined threatening to stamp the new nation out of existence. Israel, nevertheless, won that war against overwhelming odds, and Jews began arriving there from all over the world. Between 1948 and 1980, about 1.8 million migrated to Israel, many of them to escape persecution in their home countries.

God's Word is being fulfilled in all areas of life. The day of the wedding of the Lamb has not been announced, but all signs point to the return of our Lord for His bride. It's an exciting time to be alive! Prophecy is taking place under our very noses! Really, who can doubt that Life is a Great Adventure?

Union

I stood at the door of the packed-out church. All had been made ready for the wedding. The music was appropriate. Candles were lit, and members of the wedding party had taken their places. Gerald and Charles, my unpredictable brothers, were appropriately suited up, and they successfully rolled down the streamer upon which I would walk. Daddy was there, nervous, with the Minister's Manual in his hand. Betty, my sister had taken her place as my maid-of-honor, and Folger, Russel's brother, had come to represent the West family and be the best man. Those very special notes of the march sounded for me to begin my walk down the aisle toward the other most-important person of the wedding—Russel was there at the altar waiting for me.

We exchanged our vows and pledged to love and honor one another until death should part us. We took this important step in life not knowing what the future might hold, but it never occurred to either of us that our marriage might not "work out." We had committed ourselves to be faithful to each other "in sickness and health, in poverty and wealth, in the good that would brighten our days or in the bad that might darken our ways." This was the most decisive step either of us would ever make other than that of receiving Christ as Lord of our lives.

In reality, accepting Christ as Savior is not unlike a wedding ceremony—that too has to do with vows. Years before, Jesus had given me a personal invitation to become acquainted with Him, and I had decided to accept His terms for that fellowship. A relationship with Him meant the renouncing of all other loves. "We'll sit in communion together," Jesus told me, "and eat of the Word. We will be refreshed as we drink of living water." When I exchanged my vows with the eternal Son, God's Word declared that I became a child of God and a member of His royal family. I confessed my loyalty to Jesus and invited Him to be Lord of my life from that day forward. It was a life-long commitment. The vows were not made to be broken. I had done what God told me to do, and He assured me that my decision was recorded in heaven in the Book of Life.

Before saying our vows, Russel and I had been responsible for ourselves; now we would be responsible for each other. We sat down and went over our budget. On one side we listed receipts and on the other we listed expenditures. We were determined to make it financially, but it would take some close budgeting, so at the top of our "expenditure" list, we put "tithes." Separately we had learned the blessing of giving God a tenth of our income, and we knew that tithing was important to have God's blessings on the material as well as on the spiritual aspects of our lives.

Before our wedding we had pooled our money and bought a small trailer house already on Southwestern campus—and I do mean "small." The bed at the end filled the full width of the inside space, and it was just fine for Russel's height. His brother, however, stayed with Russel in the little home we would live in when he came for the wedding. He was taller, and after one night on that bed, he got up with a crick in his neck! I don't think Folger was very impressed with the sleeping arrangements Russel had made for his bride!

Camp meeting and Annual Conference came along, and we were asked to take the pastorate of the Chickasha church. Russel had bought an old Packard from one of the students who was a mechanic of sorts, and he guaranteed that the engine would be like new when he finished with it. It was barely out of his garage when we got in it to make the fifty-mile drive to our first Wednesday night service. We were embarking on a new adventure with the Lord!

We took it easy at first...35 mph...40 mph...45 mph. It seemed to be doing okay, so Russel pushed it on up to 50. Then, all of a sudden there was a loud pop, some incredible noises and rattles, and we found we could now go a maximum velocity of 10 mph! Our only alternative was to turn back toward Oklahoma City (since we were barely out of town). We stopped at the first filling station (that's what they called them back then) and called a church member in Chickasha. We were so sorry we couldn't make it that night, but without fail we would be with them for the Sunday services. What a way to begin our first pastorate!

"We won't be able to pastor this church," Russel said, "unless we have a dependable car." How could we possibly buy a car without any money? Russel soon found what he was looking for—a good-looking, not-too-old, low mileage Chevrolet that seemed to be in great running condition (and that proved to be true!).

Russel had made friends with a brother in Purcell, and that blessed man had faith in the young preacher. He said, "Russel, I'm going to do what I really don't do. I'm going to sign for your loan. I know you won't let me down." That man will surely receive his share of all that Russel would later accomplish for Christ.

We went to Chickasha on Saturday and made contact with Brother and Sister Leonard. "We have a little apartment here for you if it will help," they said. One room was a living room, bedroom, and dining room combined. The kitchen was inset from the small hall, and it was the width of the little bathroom that was just behind it. But basically, everything we needed was there to make it possible for us to go down on Friday evening, do the pastoral work necessary, have our services, and return after Sunday night service.

The small congregation owned a nice little building with a basement for Sunday school and other activities. We were united with each other and the Lord. We were in business for Christ!

We set our goals, established our priorities, and worked out our strategy. We would go to Chickasha on Friday, have our prayer meeting that night, spend Saturday in visitation, and on Sunday we would have Sunday school in the morning, youth service at 6:30 p.m., and Sunday night evangelistic service at 7:30 p.m. And oh, yes, on Saturday afternoons we would have a street service close to the post office where the "spit and whittle club" gathered. These elderly men had nothing more important to do than to sit in the sun and pass the time of day. But those Saturday services were all the church some of them knew.

Our congregation was small. On that first Sunday morning, we had a total of sixteen people! The two of us, the Leonard family, two dear elderly ladies who were sisters, the McClure family, and another sister made up the total of our church. It was always almost service time as we drove into Chickasha on Fridays, so we would begin to pick up people for the service—this was just about everyone except the Leonard family! (Brother McClure worked out of town a lot.) But God blessed us, and the little congregation began to grow.

When we visited one dear sister, Russel made special rapport with her husband. This elderly man had quite an ensemble of instruments. He played the harmonica without having to use his hands while he hit the drums and cymbals with his hands and feet. No one had ever interested him in God or the church, but Russel found his soft spot. "Wouldn't you like to serve the Lord with those instruments?" he questioned. Tears came into the old man's eyes, and he nodded. Russel led him to the Lord, and they moved his instruments to the church. Over and over again through the years, I saw Russel win such people—husbands of our lady members who previously had never been a priority for other pastors. Russel reached them, because he had a passion for people who were lost.

Russel graduated from Southwestern College at the end of that spring semester. The class he had on the "Life and Letters of the Apostle Paul" was a lifesaver—his sermons to the Chickasha people were highly seasoned with the work and ministry of that great man of God. Pastoring responsibilities and classes at Southwestern had not been easy. There were the exams, the daily homework, and the end-of-the-year thesis, but his ministerial preparation was important. He had attained an important goal and had graduated with his degree.

Our time in Chickasha had been fruitful, but of course we couldn't count success in monetary terms. Money-wise, when we averaged everything out at the end of the year, we had just about broken even with the weekly fifty-mile drives to and from Southwestern. Offerings at the beginning had indeed been very limited but had strengthened as the church grew. We had learned a lot of things. We had been faithful; we had a group of people who loved one another, and our ministry had been fruitful and had grown. Many of the old gentlemen down by the post office had received the Lord, and that group counted Russel as their pastor. During that time, he conducted the funeral for one. We knew that bearing fruit was possible only because we were in union with Christ.

Conference and Camp meeting time rolled around again. We were asked to take the church in Houston, Texas, which was under the care of the East Oklahoma Conference, and Russel felt that he should accept this invitation. We would hate to leave the Chickasha church. We were averaging sixty in attendance and the church could now support a "full-time" pastor (if he was willing to convert the basement of the church building into a parsonage). "Full-time" never meant a big salary, of course, it just meant that you worked with the church without other secular employment. So after graduating, Russel and I were always "full-time" pastors!

Union with Christ means a fruit-bearing life and ministry, not only for those who are called into full-time ministries, but to all those who serve in any area of God's work. We are one body, and workers together for the advancement of God's Kingdom. Jesus said that following him means the multiplication of our own lives. We would be witnesses first in Jerusalem—in our own hometown and reaching on out to the world. "Jerusalem" is where we are—so we must begin first with our families. You win one, or two, or three, and these in turn will win others.

Multiplication started with the Early Church and has not stopped, because the church is a living organism that automatically duplicates itself. The Church was successful in its beginning of throwing off the swaddling clothes of Judaism and of crossing the barriers of culture, language, and prejudice to reach the Gentile world. All roads then led to Rome, and in spite of martyrdom, imprisonment, and beatings, evangels of the gospel message of salvation reached out to others. The strategy was simple and continues to be the guiding force of Christianity: dare to be something more than just a believer, dare to become a multiplying disciple! Multiplication should be the natural outcome of one who is united with Christ!

It was natural then that the physical union between me and Russel should bear fruit; during our first year in Houston, our son, Russel Paul, was born. I unwrapped him there in the hospital to make sure he had all his fingers and toes—he was perfect! We brought him home, and Mom and Dad, who had traveled down from Oklahoma, were there to be with us that first week.

The parsonage was connected to the church, so we dedicated Paul to the Lord when he was only seven days old. There before the altar, Daddy took him up in his arms and blessed him. He asked the Lord to help him mature and grow in every area of his life—in the physical, intellectual, emotional, and spiritual. And we watched Paul mature with pride and excitement. To his diet of milk we soon added juice, Pablum (an instant cereal for babies), and then those vegetables and puddings. He learned to show us what he didn't like by blowing the goo back into our faces.

One of the most exciting things through the years has been to see new Christians grow in the Lord, and I mentally compare them to Baby Paul. I had declared him to be "perfect" at birth, but he couldn't feed himself, chew food, talk, or walk! What kind of perfection was that? That was perfection for his stage of growth. These other things would be added to what he could do as he matured. Many times we think newborn Christians should be born mature, but that isn't the way it works. These new believers who are saved can be sanctified and enter into a perfect relationship with Christ, but it doesn't mean that they (or we) won't make mistakes in this new life. So we have to remember that they are just babies in the Lord and feed them a diet that will help them grow and be happy Christians.

Very small children can be creative and inventive. I will never forget my horror when I found that Paul had pulled out the drawers of the desk in the living room, used them as steps, and was crowing from the top! Young Christians should be allowed to try their wings! We must help them develop their gifts from the very beginning. Small tasks come first, so that they can establish their commitment to Christ and the church. I found that many whom I solicited as helpers in an emergency did the job better than I could. It isn't always easy to discover the gifts these new Christians have. We will only learn as we are willing to give them an opportunity to be a part of ministry. They need to learn that the Christian life indeed is really a great Adventure!

While in Houston, we were asked to help get a church in Galveston started, so once a week we drove the fifty miles to have services in the home of the Branch family (what a good name to illustrate what we were doing!). The men were shrimpers; we would drive down, visit the people, invite them to service that night, and then gather together for worship. We would drive back to Houston tired, but happy to continue with our weekly schedule there. During that time, we had an evangelist who was also a builder. He and Russel drove to Galveston and back each day, got the walls up, and the roof on a new building, and came back nightly for revival services. I don't remember where the money came from to do this (!), but I do remember that the Lord blessed the services each night in Houston with renewal and outreach.

There was a group of Pentecostal Holiness churches in that area, and it was decided to begin a Texas Conference. Russel had already moved his conference membership from North Carolina to Oklahoma and to East Oklahoma and didn't feel that, as a young minister, he should make another move. So when the new conference was formed, we returned to Oklahoma and finished out the year in Henryetta since that church was without a pastor.

"We need you in Cushing," we were told. There was a nice building with just a handful of people, so we stepped in with our youth and enthusiasm to see God move again with growth and outreach. One event that stands out to me was the Vacation Bible School we had just after taking that assignment. We didn't have much money, so we made dolls with practically nothing. We filled milk bottles with sand, made the heads out of crepe paper, painted on the faces, gave them hair for girls or boys, and dressed them to represent different nations of the world. We had a missionary theme. We had covered the neighborhood with invitations, and kids came from everywhere. By the time the week was over, we had almost doubled in attendance. You can never, of course, keep everyone, but we made contact with several families who became a part of the church.

During that year, we learned a very important lesson on prayer. We were called in the wee hours of the morning. A man, whom Russel had recently won to the Lord, was very sick. Could we come? The people next door had also been contacted, so we decided to go together. We joined hands first for prayer, however, and as we finished, we all felt a wonderful sense of peace and remarked on it. "He'll be all right," we decided. When we drove up, a member of the family met us at the door. "He just slipped away a few minutes ago," she told us. God taught us a lesson on that occasion. He has different ways of giving healing. At times healing is instantaneous. People need to see these healings to know that God is at work among us. Sometimes healing is gradual. We receive by faith what we can't see or feel, but then we realize that the work is done. God did answer that prayer of faith. On occasions, physical healing doesn't happen. Many people get sick and die, but if they die in the Lord, they have just stepped over into the presence of the Lord where there is no pain, sickness, or death. That, too, is healing. This will give you great comfort when death comes to your loved ones if you know they have died in the Lord.

I believe that the "prayer of faith" saves the sick and that the Lord raises the person up, so I never feel inhibited about praying for healing. At the same time, if God reveals to me that this person is near death, it is my responsibility to speak words of comfort and peace to members of the family. God was preparing me and Russel each step of the way for a ministry of faith, healing, and revival.

After our special one-year assignment in Cushing, we decided to do a year of evangelistic work. "We just have Paul," Russel said, "and we need to know how to understand things from the evangelist's point of view." So we marked up our calendar, holding campaigns in different areas of the nation. We bought another comfortable little mobile home (much larger than the one we had started out in!), so we were "at home" wherever we were during that year. Russel became well known as a dynamic preacher and evangelist, and God blessed us wherever we were invited to minister.

During that year, I learned that we were to have an addition to our family. A couple of weeks before our baby was due, I went to Ponca City to be in the home of Evelyn (my sister just older than me) and Hollis Thurmond, her husband. Before the two weeks were up, however, our little girl decided to make her appearance. Russel, who was in a revival in Ada, Oklahoma, was called as soon as we decided that this was really "it," and he arrived just in time for Kathy's birth. (Her full name is Kathryn Joy.) Paul looked over her crib in awe; he was three years old and now he had a baby sister!

When the Lord said he would make us to become "fishers" of men (plural), he didn't want us to have just one spiritual son or daughter. Couples of the Old and New Testaments mourned when the mother was sterile and couldn't have children. Many are mentioned—Abraham and Sarah, Isaac and Rebecca, Elkanah and Hannah, Manoah and his wife (parents of Sampson), and Zachariah and Ana (parents of John the Baptist), just to mention a few. So we were indeed happy when our little girl came along. (Among the Hispanics with whom she and her husband now work, she is known widely as "Alegría" which means Joy.) She has lived up to her name!

When Kathy was just a few weeks old, Russel was asked to fill-in as the temporary pastor of Evangelistic Temple in Tulsa, Oklahoma, while the resident pastor took a leave of absence. This gave us an opportunity to get accustomed to having the new baby and be settled a bit. Very soon, however, the pastor resigned the church, and the people were in need of a full-time pastor. They asked us to remain to pastor the church. Russel was only twenty-seven years old, and this, at that time, was one of the largest churches in our denomination. We learned more during our two years at Evangelistic Temple than we could have learned in any university course! We were following in the steps of a very successful pastor—one known on radio as "Mr. Personality." We had people attending our church from Oral Robert's Abundant Life ministry. Oral and his wife, Evelyn, were members of our church. The children of T.L. Osborn sang in our choir (led by Lonnie Rex), and the Osborns were with us at times when they were in Oklahoma City.

Shortly afterward, however, the previous pastor returned and began an independent church. The first Sunday we lost nine of our Sunday school officers and teachers, and this was quite a chunk out of our congregation! One older minister in whom we had much confidence gave Russel counsel. "Don't ride a sinking ship, Russel," he said, "you are too young in the ministry. It might be better to step aside and let another more mature minister take the helm of this vessel." Russel listened to this counsel, but he had to hear from God. After all, he was not working for men, but for the Master. He began to fast and pray, and one morning the Lord spoke to him. "Stay where you are," the Lord said, "I am with you, and I will run defense for you. I have a job here for you to do and it is not yet finished."

So we stayed, and Russel now pastor, began a study of every facet of the church. The weekly budget to us was unreal, and we weren't sure how the people were going to respond financially. The nine officers and teachers and their families who were not with us were not the only ones involved in the break. Many of these people had never known another pastor, and they were only following a person they had always followed. The commitment of many of them was to the man and not specifically to this particular local congregation. Russel found that the church was carrying insurance policies on people who had helped, many years before, to restore the theatre building which housed the church. Some were long gone, but the church was still carrying this expense. The pastor had had a paid secretary, and I was willing to be one without a salary until we were sure how the finances of the church would stabilize.

"I have a new secretary," Russel told Daddy, "one who can sit on my knee and give me a big hug now and then." Daddy wasn't fooled, but Mom was scandalized! (Who *was* this secretary?) "Well, she happens to be my wife," Russel said.

Members began to work with new enthusiasm; God brought in new people, and many were saved, sanctified, and filled with the Spirit. I have known Russel to fill the baptismal tank just to baptize one person who was leaving and might not have this opportunity for a long while. When we finished the year, we had only averaged thirteen people less than we had the year before! God had helped us fill the void, and the church was moving forward.

Our third child, Joseph, was born during that time. I had already said I wanted four children, and number three had come along. I had found out that babies demanded a lot of time, but they were also a great joy! Although Daddy would formally dedicate him to the Lord, I remember that the first Sunday I took Joseph to the church, Brother Oral Roberts was there and came up to me as I held Joseph in my arms. He placed his hand on my baby's head and prayed that God would make Him into the man the Master had designed him to be. Joseph therefore was doubly dedicated to God.

We had been in Tulsa two years, and it was pastoral election time. During those years, people had an opportunity to decide if the pastor should stay or if the church should have a change. (Elections had previously been every year!) It was also an opportunity for some to "campaign" a bit in favor of their favorite preachers. It was an option they had, but it could also throw the pastor a real curve about the future. We took this as an opportunity to really consider if we were to stay on, and if not, what we should do.

"We've got to hear from the Lord," Russel said. "We need to know where we can be of greatest benefit to the work of the Lord. We are under orders from God, and He can tell us what to do." Together we waited before the Lord. "I relieve you of this responsibility," the Lord told us through tongues and interpretation, "I will send you to a place where there is another job for you to do. Don't be afraid to resign this pastorate. I will give you the direction you need." Russel talked to the superintendent and told him that the Lord had indicated that we were not to continue the Tulsa pastorate. God proved Himself to be faithful, and gave the church a good pastor to follow us. They had capable leadership, and God blessed them with continued growth and outreach.

Interested friends asked us what Russel had in mind. "Nothing," Russel answered, "the Lord will take care of us and show us what to do." The Lord was faithful to His word, and we were asked to take the pastorate of a church in Ada, Oklahoma. Many pastors are not willing to turn loose of a pastorate until they are sure something else is on the horizon for them. Some actually stay on until the church dies!

Don't do it! The work doesn't belong to you—it belongs to God, and *you* belong to Him! Once you have learned to step out by faith when you can't see the way before you, you will have made a ten-league step forward in finding God's will in every situation of your life. You can know God's will. Seek Him until you find it!

> But the natural man does not receive the things of the Spirit of God, for they are foolishness to him; nor can he know them, because they are spiritually discerned. But he who is spiritual judges all things, yet he himself is *rightly* judged by no one. For *"who has known the mind of the Lord that he may instruct Him?"* But we have the mind of Christ.
>
> 1 Corinthians 2:14–16 (*emphasis mine*)

Some people have a very difficult time finding God's will for their lives, and they run from one counselor or prophet to another seeking an answer they want to hear. God's ministers can give you counsel, and the prophet can confirm God's word to you, but these are secondary sources of advice. The Lord gave a parable of ten virgins. Five of them were wise, and five were foolish. Five were foolish, because they didn't go to the primary source for their oil. They were depending on others for enlightenment. "Give us of *your* oil, for our lamps are going out" (Matthew 25:8). You can never get all you need from secondary sources: learn to go to God. He is the fountain of all the advice and direction you need! God never intended for counselors and prophets to move people around like puppets. The only thing that will keep you steady when the difficult times come is the fact that you yourself know you are there in God's divine will and timing.

In Ada, Oklahoma, our fourth child, Philip, was born, and he was as welcome as our first. One day the pastor of the United Methodist Church stopped by and congratulated us on our new baby. When he asked what his name was, I told him. With a grin, he asked, "Oh, is he named after the Philip who sprinkled the Ethiopian eunuch?"

My response was quick, "*No!*" I said, "He *baptized* that man.*!*"

My family was now complete. The children were stair-stepped, and as they grew up Paul led the boys—in fun and also in mischief! We bought property just inside the city limits of Ada, and Russel subcontracted the building of our new home. We were on several acres and the back was like a "sunken garden" with a little stream. Joseph sat down there hours at a time, and the only "fish" he ever caught were crawdads (the only thing there was to catch!), but he enjoyed it. We had an old bell that had come out of a school Russel had attended in North Carolina, and when the kids heard it, they knew they were supposed to come to the house. If the boys delayed in coming, however, I would send Kathy to remind them, but Kathy's only authority was delegated! I told her she would have to begin by saying, "Mama said…!"

As God's children, our union with Christ also gives us authority. I think of this authority as that which a husband and wife share. When Russel and I married, we opened a joint bank account. In those early years there was never a very big balance, but we did business with that account. We gave our tithes by check, and we paid the bills and bought what we needed by check. With that little book in my purse I could go anywhere in town, write a check (if money was in the bank, of course), and sign it—Mrs. Russel B. West. My union with my husband gave me the authority to use his name and to do what needed to be done for our household. Our union with Christ has also given us authority to use the name of Jesus. He instructed his disciples:

> Whatsoever you ask *in My name,* that I will do, that the Father may be glorified in the Son. If you ask anything *in My name,* I will do it."
>
> John 14:13, 14

> Until now you have asked nothing *in My name.* Ask, and you will receive, that your joy may be full.
>
> John 16:24

> And these signs shall follow them who believe: *In My name* they will cast out demons; they will speak with new tongues...
>
> Mark 16:17

My marriage to Russel gave us four children—three sons and a daughter. What about our spiritual descendents? Russel was a soul-winner, and we worked together to help establish new people in the church—the home for God's people. I believe in the church. Jesus said, "On this rock I will build My church, and the gates of Hades shall not prevail against it" (Matthew 16:18). Some people feel that it is enough to receive Christ as Savior without what seems like an unnecessary responsibility for them. I don't believe people are complete until they become part of the body of believers.

God did some wonderful things for us during our pastorate in Ada. The church grew. We had a radio broadcast and weekly outreach through different ministries. I worked a lot with the youth and was a part of our teaching team in three different rest homes each week. I would give the class for those able to move into the open "living" area, and the others would go room-by-room and minister. I realized later that this was a very important part of my ministry development.

The Apostle Paul calls us the "body" of Christ and members in particular of that body. We are responsible to function according to our place in the body, and our interaction is with every other member of the church. Through us, our Lord has a mouth to speak, ears to hear, hands with which to minister, and feet to go where he commands. Through the years, I have observed those who work alone, and the sadness I have is that they have very little spiritual posterity. If you are in union with Christ, you will be a part of His body—the church. This does not mean, of course, that a person shut in and confined to a bed cannot be a vital part of the church. Many are invaluable as intercessors, telephone ministers, etc. To the shut-ins, God's people are commissioned to minister in a special way. Those confined to their homes or in rest homes are also a part of the church, and we must not forget them! Throughout the world people gather together, some in underground churches at the risk of their lives, but they need the strength of other members of the body of Christ.

We have freedom in the United States to worship God and to meet publicly, but we are often the targets of the media and a justice system that is doing everything it can to stamp out God's principles of holy living. Only the universal and militant Church of the Lord Jesus can hold back the tide of evil. Be a part of something that began two thousand years ago and is still going strong! Be a part of the Church! Find a congregation that bases its beliefs on God's eternal Word, and where the Holy Spirit moves with His presence and power.

As the member of a local body of Christ, the church in your community, you are a winner! Belong to the Church! Take advantage of this opportunity to leave footprints on the sands of time! It is truly a great Adventure!

Extension

It was very early on a Sunday morning of March 1960. Philip usually woke me up early for a bottle, but a deep sleep seemed to have fallen upon the parsonage family. I felt an urge to slip out of bed and into the den for a quiet time with the Lord. When I dropped to my knees to pray, God opened the floodgates of my spirit, and I began to speak in tongues. I have likened this feeling to what you would experience when you put your finger over the mouth of a bottled soft drink. If you shake it, the pressure builds up, and when you lift your finger, out will come that liquid!

There were tongues followed by interpretation, more tongues and more interpretation.

"I hold you in the hollow of my hand," the Lord told me. "I have called you, and I have ordained you. I will take you to many nations; I will be with you." I had a vision. I saw myself alone going south—a small figure in a map on a screen—going down through Mexico, on through Central America, and to the northern part of South America. I saw no borders and couldn't tell if I was in Colombia or Venezuela, but as I walked my small figure got bigger, and from upper South America it filled the whole screen.

This was the first indication I ever had about having any public ministry in the church beyond teaching. What was it the Lord wanted me to do? Here I was a young mother with four children and a wonderful husband. We worked together as a team. I had sense and maturity enough to understand that whatever I did would be at the side of my husband. But although Russel was a very missionary-minded pastor and pushed missions in the church, he had no call to missions. In fact, I remember his telling me about a girl he had met before he met me. "I would have dated her," he said, "but she is called to be a missionary. I would never do anything to hinder a person from fulfilling such a call, but I have no call to foreign missions. I could never learn another language; I have enough problems with English!" (Interestingly enough, that girl never did go as a missionary. God was saving me and Russel for each other.) But I didn't feel free to tell Russel (or anyone else) all that God was saying to me. Russel knew that God had done something tremendous on that Sunday morning, and when I couldn't seem to leave the altar after church, he whispered in my ear that he would take the children for lunch. I could return in the other car when I was ready.

If I couldn't tell my husband all about this, what was my next step? What did the Lord want me to do *now?* Russel was quite sure the Lord was calling me to preach, but the Lord hadn't specifically *said* that I would preach. To me the preaching ministry was highly exalted, and I felt that if the Lord wanted me to preach, He would tell me specifically. I was ready and willing to do whatever He wanted me to do. Like Mary, I said, "Be it unto me even as Thou wilt," and like Mary I hid the things God had revealed to me in my heart. I knew that He would let me know what He wanted me to do in His own time.

So even though I had entered into an entirely different spiritual dimension (in fact, at times I felt I was walking six feet above the ground!) I struggled concerning God's specific will in my life. Actually, I told the Lord that I was doing just about everything except preaching and being a missionary! There were days of fasting during the following months, and I felt I practically lived on my knees seeking the Lord. Then in September, Daddy was preaching a revival in our church, and the Lord laid me out on the floor. In my spirit I said, "I'm not getting up from here, Lord, until I know what You want me to do."

Again the Lord gave me those precious words that have encouraged me through the years, "I hold you in the hollow of my hand," He said. "You will preach my Word. You will speak the words I put in your mouth. I have called you; I have prepared you; I have ordained you. Fear not, I will be with you wherever you go." Since I had the Lord's attention, I had a very important request. "Lord, the only thing I ask is that you anoint me. If you anoint me with your Spirit, I will not be afraid to stand before your people and minister." The Lord gave me that assurance, and He has been faithful to fulfill His word to me through the years.

I testified immediately to my call, and at the next District Conference, I applied for minister's license. I began my ministry there in the Ada church, and it seemed to mature over night. Actually, it had been developing over the years. As Daddy's assistant, my college work at Southwestern, and working alongside Russel—these had all prepared me for the ministry I would begin.

"She won't be a preacher," one dear old grandmother of the church said, "she isn't assertive enough." And they answered back, "Wait until you hear her preach, Grandma!" The next time I preached, Grandma was able to be there to hear me, and she witnessed to God's anointing on my life. Brother K.R. Jones, one of the elderly ministers, asked me to set aside one Saturday night a month to preach in his church, and soon I was receiving invitations from other ministers in the district to share.

Russel was very sensitive to the work of God in my life. I knew *he* was the pastor, and if he wanted me to speak, he would let me know. I never told him I had a message or wanted to have the pulpit at any time, but he always knew. Sometimes he would say, "Honey, I just can't seem to find the Lord's message for the service. Do you feel He has given you something for the people?" It never failed. And during that time, I just put the things about my call that I didn't understand on the back burner.

I began to hold mini-campaigns in the district and to fill in for pastors who had to be gone from their churches for some reason. I was preaching a week's revival in Stratford on one occasion, and on Wednesday night I had gone alone because I didn't make a habit of taking our people away from the home church on a service night. But I delayed returning, and Russel was concerned about me. I was glad he had held me up in prayer. He asked me about the service when I came in. "Yes," I said, "several received the baptism of the Holy Spirit, but the lengthy service wasn't the only thing that delayed me! About midway on the return trip, I had a flat. I pulled into a service station that is the only one on that whole road. I was right there at it, but it was closed. The owner's house was set back a way, and I felt the only thing I could do [at about 11:00 p.m.] was to knock on that door and see if I could get some help! The man was gracious to me and changed my tire." When I went to pay him, though, I discovered that my money had all been used up! "Sir," I said, "I'll be coming back by here tomorrow afternoon. Please be assured that I'll drop in and pay you!" And I assure you that I didn't forget!

I must say that previous to my call to preach I was a good driver and went wherever I needed to go to take care of my household and church responsibilities, but I didn't do much driving out on the highways or at night (other than to and from church services). I would relieve Russel now and then on long vacation trips back to North Carolina, but it was really less tiring for him to drive than to try to rest a bit and keep the children in check at the same time. So, the Lord had to perform a miracle for me to feel comfortable driving to different places at all hours.

I must assure you that I considered my home and family my highest priorities. Most of my services were within easy driving distance, and Russel and I always had someone to help us in the home if both of us had to absent at the same time. The Ada church had grown, and God's power moved among us. One extended revival with Rev. Dan Beller began with an all-night prayer meeting and went on for weeks. The pastor of one of the churches in the city clapped Russel on the shoulder later and said, "Thanks, Russel, for that revival. A number of my members visited your church during those meetings and got saved!" God put it in Russel's heart that 100 people would find the Lord, and each night the number on the front of the pulpit changed. We had Sunday school classes everywhere except in the baptistery! We needed more ample facilities.

When Russel talked to the church board, he discovered that none of the men were in favor of moving to a different location. *God had given them that property at Seventh and Cherry.* So Russel took the next step and got an architectural drawing for building another sanctuary by the side of the old one. A contemporary façade could unite the two and there would be room to carry on a program of continued growth. This, too, was turned down.

Russel went before the Lord with his problem. He had no desire to gain "glory" for building a new sanctuary. As he sought God, the Lord encouraged him and renewed a promise he had given him as a young Christian. "I am going to let you go to the Holy Land," the Lord told him. It was 1961 and Dr. R. O. Corvin was taking a group to Israel. Russel would need $1,000 to go. We put together a cookbook with recipes the ladies of the church gave us and sold them all over town. Russel gave a nice Bible to the person selling the most books, and we netted $1,000 with the project. Russel got to make that trip, and I stayed at home with the "stuff"—preaching in the services and on radio, visiting the sick, and caring for the needy.

I learned a very important lesson that had to do with his return. While he was gone, we decided to redecorate his office—new drapes, new carpet, etc. I was working hard, and time was running out. We would barely finish in time for his return. I knew exactly the time their flight would touch down in New York. From there Russel would return by car bringing with him others who had shared with the expenses of that part of the trip. I thought I had calculated things correctly. Russel never ever drove all night long. I thought I knew just about what time he would be back, but I didn't realize that he would have a brother in the car who liked to drive at night and who was very anxious to return. So I was not at home when Russel drove in. When I got there, the car was in the driveway. I had missed giving him the homecoming I had wanted to give. I had been so busy working *for* him, that I had *missed* him!

Jesus did not tell us when He would return, but He promised to come. We see all the signs that proclaim the nearness of His coming, and He said He might come at any time of the day or night. "Be ready," He exhorts us, "for you don't know the day nor the hour of my return." Let us not get so caught up in working *for* the Lord that we fail to spend time *with* Him and miss Him altogether.

We had enjoyed our pastorate in Ada, but Russel was a man of vision and was not willing just to mark time. We had read some little books that were faith inspiring during that time, and we learned to set definite, reachable goals for every area of our lives—spiritual, ministerial, and material. We did this at the beginning of the New Year and would check things off our list as the year progressed. If we were not moving forward, Russel was not afraid to step out by faith and make a change. If the leaders of the church didn't share his vision, some other pastor would be able to minister to them. (Years later another pastor built a beautiful new facility and moved the church to another excellent location.) At that precise time of our history, however, we received a call to pastor the Central Church in Oklahoma City. Russel shared his vision for the church with them, and we decided to accept their challenge. The move was more important than I would ever have realized at that time.

Church growth principles tell us that long-term pastors usually have results that are more lasting. The General Church realized this and pastoral elections were held only when there seemed to be a need for them—if things were going badly at the church, if the pastor decided to leave, etc. Russel and I had always tried to be very sensitive to the Holy Spirit about any move we made, but we were not long-term pastors (although we were never voted to leave). As I look back to analyze, I feel that our work centered more on problem solving and rejuvenating the church. It was always a call to revival. Russel's heart was for evangelism and outreach as well as pastoring, and he continually endeavored to keep a spirit of revival and missions in the church.

Our work at the Central Church was important both for us and for the congregation. We didn't ever really see the numerical growth we wanted to see, but God was at work in other areas. One weekday morning I turned on the television and discovered that they were teaching Spanish on the Educational Channel. I was fascinated! I understood what they were teaching! And guess why? Their text was the same I had used in High School—*El Camino Real*. They invited those who wanted to study along to buy the book and be a part of the challenge, and that's exactly what I did! As

I reviewed, I got this tremendous urge to go ahead with a study of the language. When the fall semester of school started, Philip would be in Kindergarten, and I would have some free time.

I understood that the University of Oklahoma had an outstanding language study program, so I drove over to Norman one day to check things out. It was about a forty-five minute drive from where we lived. I found that it would be possible for me to enroll, but they would talk to me only on the basis of a degree, and if I was serious, I would have to take the requirements one by one. I talked to Russel to see what he thought about my doing something that even to me seemed sort of beside the point. But he said, "Well, I think if you would like to do that it would be great!" He always treated me like a queen, and he had a little saying, "What suits you tickles me to death!" A grammar review course in Spanish was a prerequisite for more advanced study, so I enrolled in that to take by extension on my own before the next semester started. (I think that was the hardest two college hours I ever earned!)

For the fall semester, I took the next Spanish course in the program—even though it had been sixteen years since I had had any classroom study! It was a reading class, and I put content, vocabulary, questions, and answers, etc., on tape (one of those big rolls—we didn't have cassettes in those days!). I listened to the recorder while I cooked and did the dishes, going to and from the college in Norman, and at any other time I had available. My teacher, who by now knew my educational history in Spanish said, "Keep doing whatever you're doing. It's working!" I was able to take ten credit hours that first semester and just go to classes three days a week.

I could see the children off to school, and Philip would go to Sister Henry's just a few doors down from us until I got in shortly after he got out of class. I was clear on things that I considered important: university classes were not to keep me from carrying on my work in the church we were pastoring, they were not to keep me from accepting invitations for ministry opportunities, and they were not to take time away from my family.

A crisis came one afternoon—the first warm day of spring. I hurriedly threw some sandwich makings into a box along with cookies and potato chips, and when the children came in from school, I said, "Get ready! I'm going to take you to the zoo!" This was always a favorite outing. We walked all around the park, listening to the recordings about the animals, and worked up an appetite for our picnic. We began then to look for the perfect spot where we would eat.

"That's a good place! Look, the table's in the shade, and it all looks great!" But on closer observance, we saw that there was a raccoon close by. "Don't worry, he'll leave," I said, "You know we just got through hearing about raccoons. They are pretty friendly to people." So we began to unpack our gear. But this raccoon didn't want us, and he charged at Joseph and grabbed hold of his leg biting through his jeans. I threw my purse at him, and he backed up while I urged the kids back into the car. We left the zoo immediately, but just as soon as possible, I called the zoo authorities and told them there was a strange-acting raccoon on the loose.

The doctor gave Joseph a tetanus shot but told me that there could be serious consequences. If the animal were found and tested positive, Joseph would have to have a treatment of twenty shots—one a day in the stomach. The church people prayed with us. Russel and I felt victory, but if Joseph contacted the animal's hydrophobia, it could possibly be fatal. We couldn't play with anything so serious. We would have to hear from God. We put things before the Lord. If the animal didn't test positive, we would believe that Joseph was uncontaminated. After the specified days, the doctor called. Yes, the animal had been found. In fact, he had attacked a dog and the dog's owner. Because the animal had acted so strangely, they recommended the treatment, but the great report came back to us! The animal did not test positive!" Our answer had come! Joseph had no reaction whatsoever. God had answered the prayer of faith and given us a victory that none of our family will ever forget. Our God had preserved our son for his own purposes.

Such activities had to be squeezed in between work at home, church, and university, so I had to seriously budget the way I used my time. When studying at home, my door was always open so the children could see me and interrupt me if they needed something—and the telephone was at hand to answer immediately any call that came in. I never missed any services (either on Sundays or through the week) to study for exams—finals or otherwise—and I continued to receive and accept invitations to preach in and around Oklahoma City.

The next semester I took twelve hours and the following two semesters fifteen hours each. A degree in Modern

Languages required a basic understanding of another Romance language, and I opted for French. Russel was aware of how hard I worked, and after I finished the final exam at the end of the semester, *he* said, "Boy, I'm glad finals are over!" Little by little, I had finished basic university requirements that I hadn't needed at Southwestern—geology, biology, a philosophy of religion course, etc. I needed another year to get in the rest of the requirements for the major in Spanish. That would include Spanish civilization and literature, Latin American history, literature, etc. But as it happened, I was not going to be able to finish up at that time.

For some time, Russel had felt that it would be profitable for the church to move to a location that would be better for the people who attended the church, and one day he came in quite excited. "I found a beautiful piece of property just off I-240 that would be an ideal location for a new church building. You can see it from the freeway," he said. The church bought the property, and Russel started on the preliminary work—the building plans, city permits, the church loan, and endless other tasks. The construction task was put under contract to John Pruitt, a member of the church, and his crew. It was an exciting time! Foundations were laid, and the walls were going up.

"My time here as pastor is up," Russel told me one day. "We love it here, and we love the people, but I feel the church needs someone else to lead them on to the challenge of the future. I have done all I'm supposed to do here at this time."

"What about the building?" I asked, and he answered me.

"It's all under contract, and the finances are taken care of. I'm going to talk to the conference superintendent and tell him he can help the church find the pastor God wants them to have to lead them on." I never doubted that we would find God's perfect will for this move, but it was a step of pure faith.

"What do you have in mind?" Brother Means, the superintendent, asked.

"I don't have any plans," Russel said, "but I know that when God speaks, He has a plan."

Before a week passed, my brother-in-law, Harold Hayes, called us from Bakersfield, California. "Our pastor is resigning, and we wondered if there was any possibility of your being available." How past understanding are God's ways! Yes, we could be available. Yes, Russel would be able to fly out and preach on Sunday. Yes, we would accept the church, but we wouldn't make the move until we finished the conference year in about three or four more Sundays. At the appointed time, Russel went on with the children and the furniture, and I went to Amarillo, Texas, to preach to the youth in their camp meeting.

At that time there was no university in Bakersfield. The only Spanish taught in the Junior College were beginning courses, so my advancement as far as a degree was concerned was on hold. I did two things, however, to give me practical advancement with the language. The church insisted that if I was going to work at least a day in the office with Russel, they needed to pay me so that I could have someone to help me in the home once a week. I got Carmen Musquez, of Mexican descent, to come. She was a sweet Christian, and we began the housework with a Psalm and prayer in Spanish. We spoke as much as possible in Spanish, but she was bilingual, so the work didn't suffer! Then I signed up to be a substitute teacher for high school Spanish. Of course, they were just the beginning classes, but at least it gave me an opportunity to keep my tongue working on those Spanish sounds.

We thoroughly enjoyed our work with the Bakersfield church. God began to bless, revival moved among the people, and the church grew. Russel made another trip to the Holy Land and this time he and Bob Clem went on around the world preaching in different mission points— from Bakersfield to New York and on to Europe, Israel, Africa, India, and back through Hawaii before returning to Bakersfield. Again, I stayed by the "stuff," but I told him that he must not leave me behind the next time! I not only had the church to take care of this time, but also the weekly television program that was aired on Sunday mornings. He was gone almost a month.

A highlight of this pastorate was to have a General Christian Education Convention in Bakersfield. "The church population is too thin to have a good convention in California," he was told. But Russel was adamant. He got motel and convention center prices, talked up Disney World as a vacation side trip, and promoted an attendance competition with the northern conference. He was quite determined! The people on the West Coast always traveled

East or Mid-West, why shouldn't there be a conference that more of the lay people of the West could attend?

Well, Russel won his argument, and we had that convention in Bakersfield. At that time of the year, it is usually hot enough to fry an egg on the sidewalk, but God just covered us with His clouds during the convention. Everyone talked about the wonderful weather we had in Bakersfield. (And I just smiled and nodded!) The convention was well attended, and in itself, it was a great blessing. It was well put-together and dynamic, and as the years have gone by, people still remember and mention it to me. One night at the beginning of a service, Russel took me by the hand, and we went high up in a balcony apart to just rest. I could see that he was very tired. He had had a bout with the Asian flu some time before, and he sometimes said that he just didn't feel that he had quite regained his strength.

Vacation time for us after the convention was spent in the Redwood forest. We pulled a little pop-out trailer tent and just had a relaxing, beautiful time. The kids loved the picnics, and we followed the ranger around as he told stories of the big trees. It was great just to breathe the fresh air. We also walked up to sunset rock and watched as that great orb of fire slipped down below the rim of the horizon. I remember that going up, however, Russel had said, "Let's just sit here and relax a bit." He always seemed in perfect health, and every physical exam he had seemed to indicate the same.

The old Year of 1968 was coming to a close. Russel and I had done projected planning for the church, and plans and a new strategy had been amplified and approved by the church leadership. I had the check sheet made out that we would follow for 1969. Russel was the Southern California Conference Director for Christian Education, and he was scheduled for a meeting in Oklahoma City in the closing days of the year. In fact, he was gone from us as January 1 came in, but he would be back for the first Sunday service of the New Year. I met Russel at the airport on Friday night.

As we waited for the luggage to come around, he said. "You know I didn't feel too well while I was gone, and in Los Angeles, I had to stop a couple of times and rest on my way to the terminal to come to Bakersfield. It seems I haven't been able to really get over that Asian flu." I refused to let him handle the luggage although it wasn't all that heavy.

I felt he needed to get to the doctor, so I said, "You know Paul went to snow camp while you were gone, and he sort of twisted his back. Would you mind taking him by to see what the doctor thinks?" I knew he would talk to the doctor about how he was feeling. He agreed to take him on Monday.

When Russel was gone for two days for any reason, it always seemed to take us three or four to get caught up on what had been going on. "Oh, by the way," he said, "I heard the General Youth Director say that he needed an adult to sponsor a group of young people that is going to Costa Rica in June—preferably someone who could at least speak some Spanish—so I volunteered for you. I thought that it would be nice for you to get to put your Spanish into action since you have worked so hard to learn it. I think they'll be gone about a month."

"What about you and the children?" I asked.

"Oh, we'll get someone to help us in the house," he said.

Saturday, Russel was busy tying up loose ends after his absence—calling people who had been sick and preparing for the first Sunday services of January, 1969. On Sunday night, Russel preached on how God prepares us for the future. A deep burden came over me, and I lingered around the altar, but it was still there when I went home. We got to bed, but sleep was gone from me. I slipped out, and went to a rather large closet where I could pray without disturbing anyone. I battled the burden through the night. It was something I couldn't seem to understand. Finally, in the wee hours of the morning, I said, "Lord, I know You are speaking to me about the future, and I don't understand what You are saying, but I want You to know that I put my future in your hands." With those words, the Lord gave me peace, and I slipped back into bed almost at the break of dawn. Russel knew I hadn't slept, so he whispered that he would get the children off to school. I didn't stay in bed too long, but Russel left me a note. He would be in his office at the church. I called him and said, "Don't forget that you are to take Paul to the doctor!"

Russel came back a little late in the evening. "Well, Paul will be all right," he said, "and the doctor gave me something for indigestion. Our appointment was a little late for more than just a once over for me."

We had a youth rally at the church that night, and Russel was there to open the service and give a welcome to the pastors and people who had come. Then he slipped down to the City Hall to give the invocation for the installation of the new mayor. He was back then to shake hands with the people at the church as they left the building. When we got home, we turned on the 10:00 p.m. news, and sure enough, the installation service had been televised. I was tired, and I think both of us dropped off to sleep after the "together" prayer we always had.

Something woke me up before 5:00 a.m. The light in the bathroom was on, and Russel was coming back to bed. "Have you been sick through the night?" I asked.

"No, I just woke up feeling upset at my stomach." He got back in bed, and his hands and feet were like ice.

"Shall I call the doctor?" I asked.

"No, just let me rest," he said. But I got up, went into the kitchen, and called three people of the church to pray.

"Shall we come?" they asked. "No, he just wants to rest."

When I asked him if there was anything I could do, he just said, "Don't turn out the light." They were Russel's last words, and I took them to be prophetic. The heart attack he had was massive. He no longer breathed in. His breath was going out—sort of like you would hold the mouth of a balloon while the air just gradually empties. I immediately started trying to call the doctor and the ambulance. The operator held the line open. Paul heard the activity and got up, staying on another line while I got into some clothes. It seemed to take forever for the ambulance to arrive—in fact after some time had passed, they called back to confirm that they were still needed! The doctor met me in the emergency room, and he did what he could, but I knew that Russel had already gone.

In fact, during his last moments, it seemed in my spirit that I made the heavenly trip with him. Years before at Emmanuel College while he was in the boy's prayer room before the Lord, he had an out-of-the-body experience. I never heard him tell it more than two or three times in our work, because he said people didn't understand it. (There has since been a great deal of research in this area, and no one now doubts the validity of these experiences.) He actually felt his spirit leave his body, and he was being carried in the arms of Someone whose face was too bright to look upon. He could look back down and see his body kneeling there in the boy's prayer room. He was carried through the atmosphere and into the heavens above into a place of indescribable beauty. What impressed him was that everyone he saw was young. People were wading in a crystal river, and he seemed to know everyone he saw. The trees and grass were a beautiful fluorescent green. Everything was full of life. It's true, he thought, eye has not seen nor ear heard of the beauty of this place.

Suddenly, Russel realized that he was going to be taken back to earth, and he clung to the Lord, saying, "Please let me stay here. I don't want to leave this beautiful place."

"Your job on earth is not finished," the Lord told him, and down through the atmosphere again they went. Russel saw this blue planet Earth in its beauty—just like those pictures that were sent back to us from the moon, but as they came nearer, he saw something else. He saw the continents made up of teaming multitudes. Nearer still they came, and he saw a tremendous serpent that was winding its way through the people. "That is your enemy," the Lord said. "He is a liar and a thief, and his job is to steal, kill, and destroy. He is the one you are to stand against. I have come that all who will may have abundant life."

The Lord placed Russel at a crossroad, and he was told to point the people to the narrow road that went toward Christ and abundant life. Below the road was wide and teaming with untold numbers of people. Some were sad and others were laughing. Some seemed to walk in wealth, while others wore the rags of poverty. They were literally pushing each other down this road, and from where Russel was standing, he could see a line that was drawn before a great canyon drop off. When people crossed the line, they seemed to understand what was ahead and tried to push back, but the impact of the multitude was too great, and they pitched over into the flames of fire and darkness. Russel stood there warning the people of what was ahead, and some turned aside. He preached until his strength was gone, and still he preached until his voice gave out. He fell to his knees and even then, he continued to point to Him who is the Way, the Truth, and the Life.

"I'm sorry," the doctor said. "He was very casual about how he felt. It was late in the evening, and we didn't go ahead with lab work. But I must say, Mrs. West, that nothing I could have done Monday could have possibly prevented this." Back at the parsonage, some people I had called had come to see about Russel and had stayed. I had to tell the children. I felt I had to be brave. In fact, I felt the strength of the Lord in a very special way. The next morning as I opened my eyes, God's Word came to me. I couldn't even remember where it was found in the Bible, but those words were what I needed then, and they have been with me through the years. When it seems that the world is falling apart under your feet, just remember that "The eternal God is your refuge, and underneath are the everlasting arms" (Deuteronomy 33:27). Often in times of stress, the Lord has spoken to me with poetic words, and He did just that at this time.

"Where are you, honey," I quickly cried,
"Why just in here," he said.
"I stepped into this other room,
I was by Jesus led.

I had this appointment written down
In my little black book right here.
Written down in black and white,
Why can't you see it, dear?

I've told you many, many times
This meeting I must make.
It's really been scheduled a very, long time.
This was an important date.

I know, I didn't write down the hour,
You see, I wasn't just sure,
Of the time or date, or even how,
My orders were, 'Work and endure.'

And now, I've just stepped inside
Through the door that we call "Death."
With Christ my Lord I here abide,
I came with just a breath.

We've always known that this alone
Could cause me to depart,
But you may come tomorrow,
We're just a step apart.

(cw)

Russel's death made mortality so very real, and I would forever afterward be doubly aware that there was never more than a step between me and eternity. There were so many things to do. Relatives, ministers, and church members were standing by. New Christians couldn't understand, and one young man pounded his fist on the table, cried, and questioned why God had taken his pastor. I was not only the one to be comforted, but I also had to be the comforter. I told them about how God had prepared me for this during that night as I waited before Him in that closet, and I said to them, "I want you to remember that Russel left us all a message. They were his last words, and they are for you as well as for me. He said, 'Just don't turn out the light.' So I want you to let God's light shine through your life no matter what happens. Share it with others!"

Heaven bent low as the ladies trio sang, "I hold a clear title to a mansion that Jesus has gone to prepare." Flowers, plants, wreaths, a lei from Hawaii, and telegrams from different parts of the world came in. We put Russel's little New Testament in his hand (his "little black book right there"), but I presented that to Paul before they closed the casket. The long line of cars was tremendous...

Drive up the broad and beautiful lanes of River Boulevard,

Turn through the gates, and you will find the grave
of the man of God.

His voice he raised like a trumpet, the tones were
loud and clear,
"Repent, be watchful, be ready," He cried year after
year.

Though now his voice is silent, yet in its place there
rings
The sound of a hundred others—a message each
trumpeter brings.
From coast to coast, o'er land and sea these now
with boldness stand.
They heard his call to action; they saw his burning
brand.

The sword he brandished, brandish ye! Your burn-
ing torch lift high.
Let others hear your trumpet notes echo from sky
to sky.
Until that time you, too, shall hear that heavenly
Trumpeter say,
"Well done, my strong, courageous child, this is your
crowning day.

The grave no victory o'er you will hold, you'll join a
triumphant throng.
You'll hear the choirs of heaven sing the welcome song.
So do not weep beside this grave in the city of the
dead,
For the blessed feet of the man of God now heaven's
halls do tread.

(Selected portions of the poem, *Fight On!,* CW)

I was faced with some immediate decisions. Although I had been a vital part of the church and its ministry, I was not the pastor; I was the pastor's wife. I talked to Rev. Marlow, the conference superintendent. "The people will need a pastor. Don't worry about me. I can probably teach in the public school system while we get settled." I looked ahead at the possibility of an entirely different life, but nothing seemed quite clear.

"I've talked to the people of the church and to the conference board," Brother Marlow told me, "We would like for you to continue here at the church as pastor."

"Well, I've never been ordained," I said. "You know when the Lord called me to preach, He specifically said, 'I ordain you,' so I never felt the need to take my ordination credential."

"Well," Brother Marlow said, "as a conference board, we authorize you to carry on with all church activities, and you will be ordained at the next conference."

How could I possibly give the same quality of ministry that Russel and I had been giving together? I learned that I had to find out more about the gifts the people had and to depend on others to develop in those areas to help me do what Russel and I had previously done together…and the church moved forward. People continued to be healed, saved, sanctified, and filled with the Spirit. The church attendance continued to move on up.

Then I got a call from Clifton Turpin, General Director of the Lifeliners General Youth Department, and he said, "You know, Charlene, I'm still planning on your help with this Youth in Action Team that's going to Costa Rica in June."

"Oh, you know, I can't possibly do that now with the way things have changed for me."

"Well, Russel really wanted you to go, you know. Why don't you talk to your church board, and just see what their reaction is." At least I promised him that I would do that.

When I talked to the men, they said, "You know, Brother West really wanted you to make that trip. We have local ministers here and in the conference who can stand in while you're gone. If you want to go, we think it would be good for you!" Well, life has its surprises, and that was one of them.

I had secured a very special person to be with us in the home—Sister Abbott (the sister of R.O. and W.R. Corvin). She had not been happy in her job, and she was able to come to live with us as sort of a surrogate grandmother. She really loved the Lord, and if I was absent when someone called with a need, she was always willing and ready to pray with the people who had called. She had found a ministry, and her coming made it possible for me to carry on a work that demanded my attention at any time.

I worked hard translating a couple of sermon outlines into Spanish to take with me to Costa Rica. At least if I should be called on to preach, I wouldn't have to prepare something at the last minute. Our team stayed at the Bible Institute, and we all enjoyed visiting the churches, trying out local foods, and seeing something of what Costa Rica was like. John and Edna Parker, and their son David, were the only missionaries there at that time—the Ashfords, the other Costa Rican missionaries, were on furlough. Surprisingly enough, I did have an opportunity to preach both of my sermons in more than one church. When an opportunity came to preach a third time to the same congregation, I was glad when the Parkers appeared, and I could let John Parker take the pulpit!

As I returned home, God began to roll back the years and remind me of the vision He had given me back in 1960 when he called me to preach. I hadn't had much reason to be concerned about the missionary aspect of my vision. I had been busy developing a pulpit ministry and working alongside my husband. During that summer, we had our missionary convention and faith commitment promises. Our theme was "You must go or send a substitute." But some words kept repeating themselves in my mind. "Why can't you go?" Was it enough just to give money so that someone else could go? That was what I had always done. I enjoyed giving. I was glad to give, but how could I go? Well, Lord, you know I'm a mother with four children. The Missions Department has never sent a widow with children as a missionary. This was true, although they had sent quite a few single women. I was quite sure they wouldn't want to send me alone with a family. I sought the Lord and struggled. Was it the Lord who was talking to me, or just some suggestion that had come to my mind? One morning, after hours of struggling and talking to the Lord about this, I made a decision. I would *call* the World Missions Department, and explain how I felt. If they didn't want to send me, it would be their problem, and I would be free to continue in a ministry that was growing and being blessed.

Missions Director J. Floyd Williams was on the line. He said, "Charlene, I have known you a long time. If you tell me that the Lord is leading you to do missionary work, I believe you. How would you feel about going to Costa Rica?" Well, frankly, I hadn't thought about going *anywhere*. I really didn't think they would *send* me!

"Well, wherever in Latin America, you feel I might be needed," I said.

"You've already made rapport with the people in Costa Rica, and I think it would be a good place for you to begin. The Language Institute is there, and although you've had language study, you might feel that to be profitable." They sent me a packet of materials to fill out. I almost thought I was writing a book, but I filled out everything, and when it was ready, I sent the packet in.

Meanwhile, Brother Williams was elected bishop, and Rev. B.E. Underwood became the director of World Missions. I was accepted as a missionary, and it was decided that I would go to Costa Rica under his direction. I hadn't talked to the children, because I didn't want them to be concerned about changes that might never happen. I had to talk to them and to the church, and I spent the remaining months of the year raising my support. We visited churches, and everywhere I went people responded. We applied for passports and visas and got our vaccinations.

The hardest part was leaving Paul. He only lacked a couple of credits finishing high school, and I felt it would be better for him to have a U.S. diploma. He accepted that and stayed with my sister and her husband, Betty and Bobby

Cramp, but I knew it was hard on him. It was hard on me! How I hated to leave him.

Life was not always easy, but it was still an adventure. A year after Russel's death, I left for Costa Rica in the new Volkswagen van we had bought. We would drive it to Florida, ship it from there, and fly on in to San José. We stopped as we crossed country, visiting relatives and holding missionary services. We had to say goodbye to Mom and Dad who were pastoring in Rolla, Kansas, and to other relatives. We also reported in at our General Headquarters in Franklin Springs, Georgia. By this time all of our support was raised, we would have help in Florida shipping the van, and soon we would be in Central America.

I didn't really know what kind of ministry was waiting for me and my family in Costa Rica, but we knew that God was with us. It was a step into the unknown, but I have learned a very important lesson of life. If the Lord is with you, life is always a Great Adventure!

Ascension

In the Lord's work, we learn to live above the circumstances of life. We are not under the circumstances, but above them! Ephesians 1:3 declares that we have been blessed with every spiritual blessing in the heavenly places in Christ. Verse 20 says Christ was raised up and seated at God's right hand in the heavenly places, and that all things are under His feet. Ephesians 2:6 also affirms that we have been raised up and seated in heavenly places in Christ.

We have not only been crucified, buried, and resurrected with our Lord, but we have also been seated with Him with all the authority we need to carry on the work He has given us. That is ascension! I found that the secret of joyful ministry was being sure of where I was supposed to be and not allow the enemy to trap me with his tools of discouragement, defeat, and negative thinking. I was determined to be what the Lord declared that I was—more than a conqueror through Him!

By the time I reached Costa Rica, the Dickinsons had been there about a month. We had given them a send-off from the Bakersfield church and now they, the Parkers, and my family made up the missionary team. The Ashfords would return a short time later to complete it. We were met at the airport, and a lovely tea had been prepared for us at the Parkers' home, where we would be staying temporarily. After depositing our suitcases, we gathered around the table to enjoy the refreshments. Edna Parker glanced around and said, "Where's Joseph?" Well, where *was* he, anyway? "Go ahead and eat," she said, "I'll find him." And she did. He was right down on a corner lot in the middle of a soccer game with a group of dark-haired Costa Ricans. His blond head was easily visible in the crowd! Did my children learn Spanish? Yes, and a lot of their learning had to do with their interaction with their Spanish-speaking peers in the neighborhood and in the church.

We went to church the next morning in San Pedro, and they were celebrating the Lord's Supper. "Sister Charlene (*Hermana Carlena*)," the pastor said, "would you pray for the elements of this celebration?" That was my first participation as a new missionary. I had never prayed for the Lord's Supper in Spanish, but the words were simple, and I managed to get through the task in spite of the cold chills I was experiencing. I knew there would be many other "firsts" to experience, and surely there were!

The next morning the Parkers were scheduled to participate in a youth camp, and they gave us full freedom to be in their home. While they were gone, however, I decided that I would see what I could do about renting a house, and I started out. My van had not arrived, of course, so I had to use the bus. Surely the Lord was with me, because I did find a house that I liked that was within our budget, and I rented it. We only had our suitcases, so we would have to have furniture, etc.; by the time the Parkers returned, we had located our housing and were ready to move to our new location. While getting our furniture we had to make some adjustments—like using a little Styrofoam box for a refrigerator! Most places have some drawbacks, of course, and the drawback there was that at times we would be without water!

> I have learned in whatever state I am, to be content; I know how to be abased, and I know how to abound. Everywhere and in all things I have learned both to be full and to be hungry both to abound and to suffer need. I can do all things through Christ who strengthens me.
>
> Philippians 4:11–13

I enrolled in the middle of the cycle at the Spanish Language Institute. By this time, it had been several years since I had been in any Spanish classes, and my use of the language had been limited. By the time the half-cycle ended, I was just becoming aware of my need for more language study. I was realizing some of the mistakes I was making, and I needed to eliminate them. The best thing I could do next would be to take another semester of study there at the Language Institute.

But I also needed to feel that I was helping in the work. I had been pastoring a growing, dynamic church, and it was difficult for me just to sit down and study. I was asked to work with the young people of the Barrio Cuba church, and John Parker asked me to do some typing on a manuscript he was preparing. This was good for my Spanish, although to type in a language you are not fully comfortable in is not the easiest thing to do. When the next cycle of Bible Institute classes rolled around, I would teach music and form an Institute choir. And the pastors were nice enough to invite me to preach in their churches!

Meanwhile God blessed my work with the Barrio Cuba youth, and the pastor let us organize a weekend youth revival, Thursday through Sunday, during the first days of September. The first night, two received the baptism of the Spirit, and the second night eight prayed through to Pentecost. On Friday I received word that my father was dying; I started making arrangements to return to Oklahoma. I didn't get to go to service that night, but everything was prepared, and the revival would go on through the weekend.

My son Paul met me at the airport. "How's Daddy?" were my first words. Daddy knew I was coming, but he couldn't hold out until I got there. He had already slipped away to be with the Lord of whom he had preached for so many years. We had always been so very close, and even as I write these words I feel the great sense of loss I felt when they told me. But the mantle of anointing had fallen upon me—of the six children he had begotten, I was the one out of an ancestral line of preachers to carry on the preaching ministry he so dearly loved. I must tell you, I count it a great honor that the Lord would choose me. I am not ashamed of the Gospel of Christ, because it is the power of God for salvation to all who believe!

Soon the people had all returned to their homes, and I was left again with that great sense of ministerial and family obligation. The Parkers were watching out for the children while I was gone, but I needed to get back to them. In just a week I was back again in San José. "The revival at Barrio Cuba has continued," they told me. Yes, God was still pouring out His Spirit, but some things none of us had ever experienced were happening. Some prophecies were being given that sounded a little strange. Those specifically involved in this move began a prayer meeting in a home where there were daily manifestations of the gifts without the supervision of others who would "try" the spirits. Those people, however, continued to attend the church. The revival went on for several weeks, many people were saved, and quite a number of the young people started the next cycle of study at the Bible Institute. In the middle of the revival, however, the pastor resigned the church, and the conference board asked me to assume the pastoral responsibilities.

I was pastor, but I was also a teacher at the Bible Institute. The Barrio Cuba people were great to work with and accepted responsibility. I had a tremendous Sunday school superintendent, treasurer, director of the ministries of prayer and of mercy. I remember one Thursday morning when I had a visitor, we drove by the church. I was usually at the Bible Institute and couldn't be in the church for that prayer, but as we got out of the car, I could hear the heavenly hum of prayers being lifted before the throne of grace. No wonder the Lord was blessing our work!

The church building at Barrio Cuba had actually been constructed for educational purposes, but at the time it was our sanctuary. We decided it was time to launch out and have what God intended for us as a building. The people didn't have much money, but we began our Building Fund March—the March of Blocks, the March of Cement, a

March of Metal, etc. As we reached the estimated goals for each material, we would go on to the next. Soon there was money to begin the construction, but that would be a job for the next pastor.

My children had adapted well to living in Costa Rica. Kathy continued her study of voice and piano with the wife of one of the diplomats. Joseph had sort of fallen in love with the science department at the University where he had friends. I will never forget the time he cooked the frog in one of our kitchen saucepans. (He took all the meat off and glued the little skeleton together again!) Somewhere along the way during that time, I bought Philip a guitar. He had a natural talent for music, and a young man there would play with him while he learned his instrument. Who can put a value on a single event? As Philip developed his musical talent, it could have taken him into the world, but God reserved that talent for Himself, and in years to come, it would be greatly used for His glory.

They loved the trips we made to the beach, up the mountains, or to visit the volcanoes. They accompanied me to the services we had out of town, and they came to know and love Costa Rica and her people. Our missionary family was special, and we all loved and appreciated one another for the specific gifts with which God had blessed us. Our children were teenagers together: David Parker, Vera Lynn and Alan Ashford, Terri and Karen Dickinson, and my children had some great times together. Kathy graduated from high school and went on to the Language Institute for a year (earning college credit as she did so).

It would be impossible for me to go into detail about each church where I ministered, because my work took me to many parts of the country. I considered myself to be sort of a substitute to fill in where no one else was available, and I have always felt that to be one of my strong points as a missionary—I was not in competition with any of our national workers. One day, Pastor Pedro Murillo asked me to work with a group that had some difficulty getting to the church he pastored in Cinco Esquinas, and that was the beginning of the church in La Florida de Tibas (an area of the capital city). I would take the young people, along with the accordion, for street services near the place we would later construct our church building. We would sing, one of the young people would give the Bible story, and we would give the children a piece of candy or cookie at the close of the service.

Francisco and Luz Marina Lara lived on that street, and they were right in the line of our street ministry. They didn't want an evangelical church there, and Luz Marina petitioned against us. She would send her children to the patio so they wouldn't be influenced by the services of these "evangelicals," but she would stand there and listen and watch. Then God touched her heart; the Lord healed her, and they became powerful workers in our Costa Rican church. Later they moved to the U.S. where they planted a mother church that has reached out to plant a number of others! We never know the value of something as simple as street services with children!

The group in La Florida met in homes of a housing project, and the wall of the living room of the dwellings was the wall of the bedroom next door. We had Sunday school in the same homes, but we rotated the evening services, so the people wouldn't complain of our noise. God sent us revival in La Florida, and in the matter of a few weeks thirty people had received the baptism of the Holy Spirit. The group grew to be a congregation. One man saw property that would be a good location for a church, and he assured the owner that we could pay him his down payment immediately and give him the balance within three months! We emptied the treasuries—general church, women's ministries, youth, Sunday school, etc., to be able to pay the initial amount.

I felt directed to write twelve people. I didn't ask for money, but I told them the situation and asked them to pray that God would supply what we needed. Not all of them responded with a monetary offering, but I knew they would all pray. Some gave far more than I could have expected! And by the time the three months were over, we had the money to pay for the land! We learned city planning called for a street to go right through the middle of our property to connect it with another addition. We would have to have that street in to be able to get our plans approved. So God just gave us another miracle! The city itself put the road through for us! It was time for me to give up that work, but God gave us a builder and pastor combination—the land was there and the site was approved for building the church. Today that building, with its enlargements sits on the property God gave us for the glory of the King. (They later built a house for a parsonage on the other side of the new street.)

My son, Paul, had had a life-changing experience with the Lord and he and his friend, Orlando, drove down from the U.S. through Central America in a Volkswagen microbus. We all explored Costa Rica again with them, and we decided to make the return trip to the U.S. together—in the VW microbus! As we traveled the Pan American Highway, we would claim those people for Christ and His Kingdom!

It had been so orchestrated by the Lord that there was peace in Central America at that time. We loaded up as lightly as possible with six in the vehicle, and it was an unforgettable experience—through Managua, Nicaragua, just about six months after a devastating earthquake, and north on the Pan American highway…through parts of Honduras and El Salvador…and finally reaching Guatemala. We spent the nights in the capital cities, visiting their markets, eating local foods (with great care!), and enjoying places of national interest.

We would never forget our time in Guatemala City, and on to Antigua, with its ruins of a tremendous Sixteenth Century Spanish civilization. There in the central market, we saw the little Indian women cooking tortillas over their small grills and in the background there stood those magnificent columns of a bygone empire! We left Antigua with the intention of returning through Guatemala City and on to Mexico by way of the Pan American Highway. We got on the right highway, but unfortunately we later discovered that we were on the wrong end of it! We were so fascinated with the beauty of Lake Atitlán and the highway that took us right around it, that we hadn't bothered to look closely at the map. We watched as the day began to decline, and the setting sun started to paint its beauty over the canvas of the sky—and reflected it all in the surface of that beautiful lake!

We should have reached Guatemala City long ago! A look at the map assured us that we would not return through Guatemala City unless we wanted to turn around and retrace our steps. But we could actually cross the Mexican border by the highway we traveled. So ahead we went. Most of the little villages we passed didn't seem to be on our map! We assumed that we were on our way to the Mexican border, and we would stop and ask about where the border was. "*Recto! Recto!*" (Straight ahead!) they would answer back! No matter who we asked, the answer each time was the same. We found no possible place to spend the night, so on we went. Following directions, we actually found ourselves once at the dead end of nowhere—in front of us was a cornfield! So we turned around, and on we went until finally, we did reach the Mexican border. What an experience!

On Life's Adventurous journey, there is only one map to follow, and there is only One Way to reach your destination. Jesus is the Way, the Truth, and the Life. If we travel with Him, we may sometimes find ourselves on what seems at the time a detour, but if we just keep consulting the Guide Book, God will lead us safely on. We may get tired, but our Lord has promised to give us the rest we need. "Come unto Me," He said, "and I will give you rest."

Traveling the length of Mexico in itself was an adventure. In Puebla, we visited our missionaries and also the pyramids there. We could go inside them, and that was a new experience as we walked those narrow passages! "We're also going to the U.S. border," our hosts told us, "for a Women's Ministries Convention." So we traveled along together, and they led the way. We stopped and ate together, visited Mexico City with all of its color, its mariachis, more pyramids, and then on north again. North America, here we come!

In Oklahoma City, we rented a house and got read-justed to life in the U.S. This furlough was to be full of important events. I usually drank a cup of tea with three different groups. Philip was in junior high, Joseph was in high school, and Paul and Kathy were at Southwestern. They all left for school at different times, and I sat down with each one as they ate breakfast. It was my little "together-time" with them. That year Paul and Terri Dickinson married, Joseph graduated from high school, and Kathy and Gary Petty became very interested in each other. Kathy and Joseph would pursue their college work in Oklahoma City, and only Philip would return with me to Costa Rica.

When I reached Costa Rica, I was asked to go back to Barrio Cuba, because the pastor had resigned. I looked over the building where construction had begun when I had previously left the church. Instead of occupying a builder who was a member of the church, they had called in a construction team, and soon the money was all gone. There the hull of the building stood—and it seems someone had prophesied that it would never be completed, because the Lord would come first. Well, the Lord didn't relay that information to me. The roof was on and the walls were up, but there were no doors, windows, floor, or ceiling. We scheduled a campaign, moved the pews from the upstairs part of the sanctuary/educational building, and began the revival. Eighty-five people were saved in that campaign, and the congregation became enthused to finish the sanctuary. Everyone wanted to do something. Children with little buckets carried sand and rocks, and the project went forward as people put their shoulders to the wheel and lent a hand. God had given me people who had a mind to work!

I truly believe in the prophetic ministry of the Holy Spirit through anointed prophets, but I do not believe that God uses them to move people around to do things he has not revealed to the people themselves. I depend on the Lord to reveal His will to me. The prophets will confirm that ministry, and there will be no doubt in my mind that it is real. When I went ahead with the building in Barrio Cuba, I had no sense of disobedience to the prophetic word—the Word told me to "try" the spirits. I was also taught to look for the Lord's coming every day, but to work for Him as if I had another one hundred years to plan for future outreach. I still believe this is the right perspective to maintain.

During my time in Barrio Cuba, I noticed that we were baptizing quite a group of people from Sagrada Familia, a community just across a footbridge from Barrio Cuba. The people walked in front of our church instead of riding the bus the long way around, and they would stop in as they heard the singing and preaching. One night Alejandro got saved (he was so very drunk he could hardly stand), and the next night he brought his wife. They were at the point of separation, but God saved their marriage and their home became the meeting place for a small group ministry. For a long time we had taken young people to the streets of

Sagrada Familia for a children's ministry, now we had the possibilities for beginning a church. My workers, along with Kaye Martin, my missionary co-worker, helped in this teaching ministry. I turned this work over to Kaye in its infancy, and she took it from that beginning. Today it stands as a testimony to the saving grace of the Lord.

I visited it years later, and a nice young man met and greeted me at the door. "Do you remember those kids who used to stand outside that house and sniff glue?" he asked. "I was one of them," he said. "Now I count it a privilege to work for the Lord right here where I grew up!"

The conference board was closing the work in Alajuelita, because the building was falling down. I asked them to let Barrio Cuba take over that ministry as we were the closest church. We tore down the old structure and built a temporary place of worship on another small piece of property the church owned. The conference superintendent and members of Barrio Cuba shared in ministering. Then, we found a piece of property, and again, God supplied the need. He helped us sell the property we had and the new land was bought with the profit. Don't ever doubt it! God is the Source of *everything* you lack in your work for Him. He will supply every need according to His riches in glory. A tent meeting was conducted on that property with different pastors and churches cooperating. The work was reborn, and it stands today as a testimony of God's grace.

A duplex was built on the Bible School property. Philip and I lived on one side and Kaye Martin on the other. Philip and I had some good times together during that time. We often sat on the front porch in the early morning and ate breakfast together while we watched the changing colors of the sky. When possible we had our times of escape to a favorite place along with some of his friends or Kaye for company. During this time, along with my work as a missionary, I wrote two books: *Making Disciples through the Sunday School* (in Spanish for the Sunday School Department), and *Close Out of the Ages* (a correlation between the seventieth week of Daniel and the Book of the Revelation). These were printed by Advocate Press.

Ascension means that in Christ I have authority. It means I don't have to be in the dumps one day, endeavor to climb on to the top of the mountain the next day only to fall again. A person simply lives in Christ, and all things work together for God's glory including the problems and difficulties. The development of a ministry means change, but I can move from one of God's assignments to another with victory. When I began my work in Costa Rica, I had no sense of being there the rest of my life, although I would have been willing to have stayed! It is indeed a beautiful country with its beaches, mountains, and excellent climate! I enjoyed the nine years I lived there.

Some of us, missionaries who had been in Costa Rica for a while, felt it would be good to step aside to see our national workers become more involved and to reach a greater degree of maturity in leadership. I asked the Lord where my next assignment would be. I had briefly toured most of the South American countries while living in Costa Rica—Panama, Venezuela, Brazil, Argentina, Chile, Peru, Ecuador, and Colombia. On that trip, I had visited missionaries and churches I knew in some of the countries as well as other points of interest such as museums and art galleries. I had stumbled over the Portuguese language in Brazil, ate local foods, and got around on public transportation in the different countries. My missionary co-worker Kaye Martin (later Muñoz) met me in Peru, and we finished the tour and returned to Costa Rica together.

But where would my next assignment be? God reminded me of the vision I had in 1960 when I saw myself going south through Mexico, Central America, and on to the northern part of South America. I informed the World Missions Department about my decision to leave Costa Rica and said I would work either in Colombia or Venezuela—I had seen no borders in my vision. I was asked to go with the Mario Gutierrez family to Venezuela, and our first event was to cooperate in a citywide campaign with a well-known Latin American evangelist. I was to leave the U.S. to begin my work the first of April as the campaign would start at the beginning of that month.

But there was a glitch in that for me, and I bolstered my courage and went for a talk with Missions Director, B.E. Underwood. My daughter Kathy and her husband Gary Petty were expecting their first baby, and I felt I needed to be with her at that time. Would it be possible for me to delay beginning my work in Venezuela until the first of May? He courteously heard me out, but with a little smile he said, "Now, Charlene, you know that you can't tell about these babies. They might come early or they might come late, and really it is for this city-wide campaign at the beginning of April that we need you." I accepted what Brother

Underwood told me. He was always easy for me to talk to, so I made my plans to leave the first of April.

Don't ever be afraid to submit to the authorities God has placed over you. He has a way of working all things out, and in so doing, He just may give you a miracle! He may see that what is important to one of his children is sufficient reason for Him to delay a citywide campaign for a whole month to give her the desires of her heart! And that is exactly what He did! "Yes," Brother Underwood said, "you may leave the first of May, but I tell you that this is the first time in my experience that a citywide campaign on a foreign field has been delayed so a mother can be with her daughter for her first baby!"

Isn't God great? Really He is, and without a doubt, it's a Great Adventure to walk with Him!

Missions Beyond

We began our work in Venezuela by cooperating in a city-wide campaign in Caracas with Evangelist Domingo Pilarte. God worked mightily saving and healing people, and we were given a share of the decision cards to work with. At the close of the campaign, Rev. Pilarte preached a week for us in a theatre we had rented. Crowds were excellent and people from different churches helped swell the attendance. We did follow-up as much as possible on the new believers—telephone calls, letters, invitations, etc. When the week was over, however, and Sunday morning service came, we had about nine people (beside the Gutierrez family and myself). We saw we would not be able to keep renting the theatre so we decided to set up our tent in a place called Palo Verde. Our campaign continued, and some people were saved who became established in their Christian walk with the Lord. Property was very scarce and very expensive, but finally a second floor hall was rented to begin our work. Regular services were started, and I was helping mostly with music on the little keyboard. This was a difficult transition for me, because I had been the pastor of a growing and dynamic church that was experiencing revival.

I was in a big city where I knew no one and was staying in a small hotel room. I had a hard time getting my mail; I wasn't hearing from my children and for the first, and about the only time in my life, I was lonely. Then I was invited by Hilario and Elizabeth Rincones to occupy a room in their home with their two daughters. They, along with Hilario's cousin, Augusta and her husband Mamerto Díaz, were my good angels. Hilario and Elizabeth and their family were faithful members of another Pentecostal church, but Augusta and Mamerto became an important part of our work.

From the beginning I searched for an apartment—going from one place to another. They were dirty, had no light fixtures or kitchen cabinets, etc.! One day, while standing with Hilario on the balcony of his apartment, he said, "Do you see those apartments there in the distance?" Yes, I saw them. "Well," he said, "Mamerto and I have an apartment each there. As soon as they are ready, you can move in! Mine is to be a rental." Wow, a brand new apartment! The rent was within my budget (I later learned that he was just asking half of what my neighbor paid!) "When will they be ready?" I asked. "I think in about three weeks," he said. At the end of those three weeks, I asked again, and the process was repeated again and over again! I was with the Rincones about three months—but I lived in their apartment the thirteen years of my stay in Venezuela. The Lord didn't let me find an apartment sooner, because he was reserving the best for me. Remember, that when one door closes, you are just that much closer to the door God wants you to enter!

During those first weeks I met Armando, Yolanda Sandoval, Bertha Sol, and others. Bertha had been saved in a Full Gospel Business Men's Fellowship and was attending Charismatic services. "I want to have Bible classes in my home," Bertha said. "I've talked to the priest, and to some sisters, and no one has time. Would you give some studies?" I was really without a ministry at that time, and I was anxious to be involved so I accepted. "I'm Catholic," she said.

"I'm evangelical," I said, "but if you are willing just to take the Bible to answer any questions, I'll come." She was interested in reaching people who, like herself, would never have knowingly attended an evangelical meeting, so she didn't want it to be identified as such. The first night, the meeting began with just her and her two daughters. For my class that night I simply used the index of the Bible to help teach them how to find the Scriptures we would later be looking up. It didn't look like a very promising beginning. However, with time the meetings grew, people from the neighborhood, and others who were invited, came and service after service people who had never invited Jesus into their lives did so. People began to be filled with the Spirit, and we baptized them in water. My hands were tied, however, about getting these people to my church. My hostess didn't want to promote an evangelical church. These people lived in a high social strata of the city—dentists, lawyers, TV commentators, etc., and our church was very much in the "blue collar" section! So other churches, already established with good buildings profited more from my ministry there than my own work did. But I had not given my service in vain. Many times I have met people I didn't even remem-

ber, who said, "Charlene, I received the Lord with you in
Alto Prado." Who can measure the value of a soul?

One night about five people from a charismatic group
attended our study, and when the meeting was over, they
wanted to have a little time with me personally. We stepped
out into the patio, and one of them said, "We just wanted
to give you a word from the Lord. You will go to Africa,
and the Lord will be with you." I took these people to be
rather new in the area of prophetic ministry, so I just listened and thanked them. I had prepared for ministry in
Latin America, and at that time, I had no leading to go
elsewhere. But I "tried" the spirits, and I didn't feel any ill
on the part of these people, so I just put their prophecy on
my "back burner."

When Rev. Elvio Canavesio, our Latin American
supervisor, visited us during the first months, it was decided
that it would be best for me to be the pastor in Caracas,
and for Brother Gutierrez to work on planting churches in
other areas. So I surveyed the situation. On paper the work
in Caracas was supposed to have had a big beginning, and
Brother Gutierrez actually had baptized lots of people in
water—but they were mostly people who had no spiritual
roots or commitment. Connie Gutierrez (Mario's wife) and
their family were a stable part of the church, and the boys
were a great help with the music. I praise the Lord for that
family, and we bonded together for the work during that
time. Hermes Quintero and Efigenia (with Junior in arms),
Manuel Herrera, and Martha Díaz were saved in the city-
wide campaign, and they and Sister Martha's family stuck
with us in the new work. Thibayre's son also received the

Lord in the campaign; she saw the change that took place in his life, and she and her family became a part of the work. The people who had been saved in the campaign in Palo Verde moved with us to the new location at the corner of Avenue Francisco Miranda and Campo Rico.

Then the Lord began to bring in others. Jorge Trincado, from the Jotabeche church in Santiago, Chile, climbed the stairs one Sunday morning with two of his brothers. He had a letter from Pastor Vazquez stating that he was to attend the new work the Pentecostal Holiness Church was starting, and he was to stay there. Jorge organized a choir, and those who sang included about half the congregation! We were just a handful of people, but the choir became an evangelistic tool. People like Bolmer and Estela heard the singing, climbed the stairs to see what was going on, received the Lord, and with their two children, became a part of our *Centro Cristiano de Caracas*. Then Bolmer saw Hernando one Sunday morning on the street. Bolmer had served liquor where Hernando had gone to drink, but that day they both had their Bibles. Hernando had just received the Lord in Colombia and was looking for a church. "Our pastor is a lady missionary," Bolmer said, "but I think you'll like her. Come along."

I had some people who were capable of giving devotionals for the prayer meetings, and to prepare them I was giving a homiletics class before service on Wednesday nights. Hernando Brochero later declared that his first discipleship classes began with a course in homiletics! (He came because his family was in Colombia and he didn't have anything else to do!)

The work branched out into other areas. First, our tent was set up in Higuerote right on the beach, and a lasting work, *Centro Cristiano de Higuerote,* was started. Later we were in Ocumare in the tent—and our *Centro Cristiano de Ocumare* was established. After that, Nueva Cua got the now well-worn tent and our work there began. I had been involved in these new beginnings by teaching doctrinal courses. Many of our people received the baptism of the Spirit during that time in those different places, because I do not believe a teaching is complete unless the people are given the opportunity to experience what is being taught. It was at this point of our development that our first conference board was elected to direct the activities of the fledgling conference. When this took place, Brother Gutierrez returned to other areas of ministry, and I was left as field superintendent of the work as well as pastor of the Caracas church.

In *Centro Cristiano de Caracas,* we had begun our Bible Institute early on. We had to do it as an extension work. The students would study and prepare their lessons, come to class once a week, and the church would serve as a place of on-the-job training. As new churches were added, we set up the same program in different areas. The studies included all that we had taught in our live-in Bible Institute in Costa Rica—but without the tremendous expenses involved in that type of project. At that time I lamented not having a facility for a live-in Bible school, but I later saw that God had directed the way we did this also.

We continued to reach out, and Caracas became a church-planting church. For two years while I was pastor of the church in Caracas, I drove on a dark, crooked, and often times rainy road to a home in Los Teques—taking people with me when possible, and going alone when no one was available to accompany me. (I usually had to leave before most people got off work.) When we finally found a place to begin the church in Los Teques, we scheduled an open-air campaign in the high school stadium. Carlos Verliac, an Argentine whom God sent to help us in the work, was the campaign evangelist, but the conference superintendent and different pastors and congregations took different nights sharing the ministry (and helping us round out the attendance in the meetings!)

Following the campaign, there were a good many people who wanted to be a part of the new work in Los Teques, and there was a week of doctrinal study to prepare them for the organization of the new church. *Centro Cristiano de Caracas* had already invested in over two years of work, and now we invested with some of our finest workers: Hernando Brochero had already helped and made rapport with the people, and now we would release him, his wife Fabiola, and their family to become the new pastors in Los Teques. Hernando had served first as a greeter at the door, and later as a Sunday school teacher and treasurer of the church. He had also developed into a dynamic preacher of the Gospel. We would miss him, Fabiola with her beautiful voice, and the children in our work in Caracas, but we knew that in God's timing to divide is also to multiply—and God proved that to be true. He led the Los Teques church to beautiful ministry. (Hernando later became pastor of the Caracas church that now numbers over 1,500 and also Superintendent of the Conference. Positions he presently holds as I write these words. I'm glad to be his spiritual Mamá!)

The World Missions Department had informed us that we could receive some money to help us buy property for a building in Caracas, and we were watching the newspapers and keeping our eyes open to see what God had for us. It was Adelciria, my co-worker from Costa Rica, who spotted the newspaper notice, and we went to look it over. The big rock house was solid with beautiful floors, but it had been abandoned. There were no doors, bathroom, kitchen, or light fixtures. Metal frames for the windows were there, but the glass was broken out and the metal had become quite rusty. The place was full of trash and obscenities were drawn and written on the walls. It was an inheritance, and the heirs had not been able to get together on it. Mamerto Díaz, now a lawyer, had the nearly impossible job of straightening things out so that we could sign the papers, but he finally did it! People set to work with a will! The first day we worked, we filled about sixty big bags of trash and wore out metal brushes scraping the rust off the window frames! The whole place had to be cleaned, rewired electrically, painted, etc. As soon as possible, we began to occupy the building as we continued to work. With a permanent place for worship, we felt we would now be better able to establish our church identity in Caracas.

At different times during my time in Venezuela, members of my family visited me briefly. Paul and his wife Terri, Joseph, and Philip came for short visits. One lady, not remembering that Philip had been raised in Costa Rica, slowly said, "Tu Ma-má, pin-ta." (*Your mother oil paints.*)

He repeated, "Mi Ma-má pin-ta!" Her daughter went into gales of laughter as she reminded her mother that Philip was bilingual!

Jonathan, my oldest grandson, spent his summer with me when he was nine, and I was amazed at how quickly he caught on to the value of money. In his way of thinking, some things were very inexpensive—especially the food at La Padova (a place he called the "Chicken Factory"). It was amazing that he would not be at all hungry before going to church, but he was really sick for something as soon as the service was over. "Can we go by the chicken factory, Grandma?" was a common request. We did a lot of traveling in the car while he was there, and we passed time by playing, "I'm thinking of a character whose name begins with a …" We would try to stump each other asking questions, and he became an expert at remembering the names of Bible characters! He was a little frustrated in the church services, because he couldn't sing the words to the songs although he knew the melodies of quite a few. "Do you have the baptism of the Spirit?" I asked him. "Do you speak in tongues?" When he told me that he did, I said, "Well, maybe you can sing those songs in your heavenly tongue!" And I noticed that he did.

Jesse, Paul and Terri's second son, spent his vacation with me when he was twelve. I remember that I was giving a Bible study in one of the churches, and they asked me to minister on the baptism of the Spirit on Sunday morning. Jesse hadn't received the promise of the Spirit, so I explained to him ahead of time what I would be saying to the people who came down to be filled. "Just come along with the others," I told him, "and believe that when I lay my hands on you and pray, you will be filled with the Spirit." What a blessing it was for me when he began to praise the Lord in other tongues. Jesse is now a fine guitarist, leads singing, and has developed a good preaching ministry. The mantle of God's Spirit rests upon him.

Then I was to be blessed by having family with me on a more permanent basis! My daughter and her husband, Kathy and Gary Petty, and my grandchildren, Lisa, Rachel, and Daniel, were coming to be a part of our missionary team in Venezuela. I did all I could to smooth things for their arrival. We had an apartment ready for them to move into, and right away I had them come to my apartment for their first meal with me. I tried to make it special and lit several candles. When I opened the door, three-year-old Daniel, seeing the candles, jumped up and down and declared that it was his birthday! Even though Kathy explained that there would be no presents, he still insisted. Maybe it really doesn't hurt anything for a little guy to have two birthdays in one year! Kathy and Gary slipped into the work, and we were able to help each other and do so much more as they took up the reigns of their ministry.

The grandchildren's birthdays were very special to me during that time. I would have the birthday girl or boy for a restaurant meal (one on one), and they could choose the place they wanted to eat. Caracas had so many special places! There was an excellent Chinese restaurant and *Le Jardin de Crepe* with its French food, but their favorite was an Arab restaurant. Daniel's reason for wanting to go there was because he could have lemonade with a stir stick and cherry!

Our next Venezuelan outreach was in an area called Jabillos and the workers we would release there were Hermes and Efigenia Quintero, with Junior of course. Kathy, Gary, and the children really helped in this work. Hermes had applied for a lot to homestead, and he also asked for a lot for a school and a church. Soon a school for children was set up. The small local school didn't have room for everyone, and this school met a specific need. Hermes has a beautiful voice, sings specials, is a good worship leader, and developed a fine pulpit ministry. He would be a capable pastor, and he was also a builder. They bought molds for cement blocks, and he worked hard making blocks for the building that would later house the church. That church and school grew and years later Hermes Jr., who had been in arms when I went to Venezuela, became the pastor, releasing his father to plant another church!

CURSUM, an Advanced Ministerial Training Course *(Curso de Superación Ministerial)* came into existence. This was to round out the Bible Institute programs in different areas of Latin America; June Carter (Canavesio) was the director and developer of this program. Along with my work as pastor and field superintendent, I became a teacher in this endeavor that took us to different countries for these studies—two areas of Mexico, Costa Rica, Venezuela, Argentina, and later Colombia.

When I left for furlough, we had our strategy check sheet prepared for *Centro Cristiano de Caracas.* The next pastor would not be obligated to do what I had planned before leaving, but one of the things on our list was to begin a new work in Guarenas. We had a number of people living there (about forty-five minutes by bus from Caracas.) When I returned from furlough, nothing had been done about Guarenas, so we started that new work. While working with the people we were able to rent a facility, and the church later occupied the rest of that building for the work.

Did you ever feel that you started something and didn't get to finish it? Well, I felt that way about the university language study I had started years before. So while on furlough, I went back to the University of Oklahoma and had everything evaluated. I could get my degree in one year if my grades would validate the previous work I had done *and* if I could fulfill the requirement of a basic understanding of another language (considered to be the equivalent of two semesters.) I had only had one semester of French, but I didn't want to repeat it. Through the years, I had reviewed from time to time, but how could I possibly take a second semester after a gap of fifteen years? "You can go in for an evaluation," they told me at OU. I decided to buy a *Living Language* course (two cassettes, a manual, and dictionary)— about $15 at that time. I immediately pushed the tape into the player as I traveled. I couldn't look at the manual and had no idea what was being said, but I faithfully repeated the words (actually, they were names of people!) I bought a Walkman and listened and responded as I walked, went to sleep listening, listened and responded as I traveled, and as I did things about the house. There are different ways of learning perseverance!

I went in for the language evaluation, and it included areas for analysis in written, oral, and comprehension. If I couldn't come out pretty good on that, I wouldn't be able to finish in two semesters. My scores surprised me: I evaluated to go into the *fourth* semester of French! With a lot of work and a $25 test, I had saved myself a lot of time and money! I had met the requirement without actually taking any more French classes!

I enjoyed my work at OU and earned my BA in modern language with distinction on May 6, 1989. I enrolled in the continuing education program for a master's degree. With a pile of books, I returned to Venezuela and did my missionary work as I studied for the MLS (Master of Liberal Studies). I was able to complete that and receive my degree on August 5, 1991.

I feel the Lord helped me choose my materials for study and the professors at OU were excellent. All of my studies, except for other degree requirements, were based on Spanish language study. That included Latin American and Spanish civilization, history, culture, literature, language, etc. The studies enriched my understanding of the people with whom I work and gave me a greater appreciation of what these wonderful people have contributed to our world.

During my time in Venezuela, I took my first trip to the Holy Land. I had seen a brochure in a Christian bookstore and refused to even pick it up—I didn't have the money available to make such a trip. The tour would take a group to New York City, on to Europe, include a trip to Turkey to visit the sites of the seven churches of Asia mentioned in the second and third chapters of Revelation , visit the Isle of Patmos, Petra, go on to Israel, and return back through Europe, New York, and again to Caracas. Bertha Sol came to visit me. "I want you to go and room with me," she said. "I'll pay half your fare." Others gave me money, and I was able to make arrangements for the rest.

Something very interesting happened! When Israeli travel agents looked at our agenda, they told us we couldn't go out of the Israel as planned. So instead of visiting the ancient city of Petra, we would visit Cairo, Egypt. It would have cost more, but we would travel from Cairo to Israel by air-conditioned bus. Hey, Egypt is in North Africa! I would have to take a prophecy off the back burner! That prophecy the charismatic group had given me would indeed become a reality! God would let me go to Africa! Little by little, God was fulfilling a prophecy He had given me in 1960 when He said, "I will take you to many lands!" Do God's promises to you sometimes seem a little far-fetched? Never fear, if they are truly from Him, they will come to pass in their own time.

But lands shouldn't be entered just to visit. Everywhere I went I claimed the people for Christ. Our church was working in Venezuela, but we needed to extend our work into other areas of South America. The Lord's commission is "into all the world!" An opportunity to be a part of another South American outreach came when Rev. Canavesio asked me to visit a group in Barranquilla, Colombia. Alvaro and Monica Castro were having services in their home, and they seemed to be interested in becoming a part of our church. They had a pretty good group, and I enjoyed meeting with them. We sat and talked about doctrinal issues, the work

they had done, their vision for the future, and the ne\
be met. After this visit and on the recommendation of o\
friends, we invited them to become a part of our church\
and Colombia was added to my list of responsibilities as
field superintendent. We also took CURSUM to Colombia,
and I visited them three or four times a year for seminars,
conferences, mini-campaigns, etc. As the work grew, the
need for a permanent location became urgent, and the Lord
let me help them find and buy the property they now own.

One day, I knew my time in Venezuela was coming to
an end. I had always asked the Lord to let me be sensitive
to His timing. "Grandma, we came here to be with you!
You can't leave us!" Daniel may have thought he came to
Venezuela because Grandma was there, but he had really
come because God had sent him and his family.

"Well, what do you think you will do?" I questioned
myself, and the enemy whispered, "You're just about sixty,
and jobs for people your age aren't hanging on trees!" I had
prayed over the countries of Latin America, and I didn't feel
urgency for any of them. I felt no direction, but I knew God
would guide me. My resignation to the World Missions
Department was a step of faith. I told them I would stay on
until the end of the year. I didn't feel direction to another
country, but I would not rule out the possibility of working
for the Department if there was something they needed me
to do. I was not interested, however, in anything that was
available at that time. I would wait on the Lord.

I taught a ministerial training study for CURSUM in
West Mexico at that time and returned through Oklahoma
City. I went to our General Offices and saw Bishop

Underwood. He had just heard that I had decided to leave Venezuela. "What are you going to do? Do you have anything in mind?"

"No," I told him, "I'm sure the Lord will give me direction."

"Come to my office tomorrow," he said. The next day he sent me to see Rev. James Leggett, director of Home Missions (now Evangelism USA.)

"I need to set up an office for Hispanic Ministries," Brother Leggett explained. "That is a growing area of the church." He was really looking for a Hispanic man who could lead the department, but when he would mention some name, there were always obstacles someone would put up. I had always felt that one of my strong points as a missionary was that I wasn't in competition with anyone nor did I take anybody's job away from them. If I didn't have a place to work, I started one. Maybe this would be a strong point for Hispanic Ministries. I was asked to begin my work the first of February 1991.

God had answered again! I had made a bold step of faith when I resigned from Venezuela, not knowing what I would do or where I would go, but before my time in Venezuela came to a close, God had given me another place to minister for Him!

It wasn't easy to leave Venezuela. These were my people. I had seen them born into the Kingdom, mature, take places of responsibility, launch out into the deep, and become workers for the Lord. Nor was it easy to leave Kathy, Gary, and the grandchildren. But the mantle of the Spirit rested upon them as well as on the national workers, and it was easier to go, because they were there to fill the void of my absence. The foundation of the work had not been laid upon a person, but upon Jesus the solid Rock!

On life's journey, we sometimes come to a turn in the road, but the highway leads onward and upward, and it's a Great Adventure when we are in the company of the King!

Missions at Home

I returned to a new job and a new life in the States for Christmas and cold weather. I had lived in semi-tropical countries for twenty-two years (except for furlough times), and it wasn't a very good time of the year to get re-acclimated. My son Philip was my good angel at this time. I lived with him in his mobile home for about three months—looking to buy a house and get resettled. It was so good to be back and have some time with him and with other members of my family.

I got established in my office in Evangelism USA at our Headquarters (now called Resource Development Center), and in time bought my house just five miles from work. Now I had my own little nest at home and a wonderful place to work. I had known many of the people employed at our Headquarters for years, and working with Rev. Leggett and the staff at EVUSA was a blessing. The position of Hispanic Ministries had not existed before, so my job was foundational. There was nothing to work with in my office, and the only statistics were those in the general files of the denomination. But I had personal materials to use as a basis to build up files—copies of letters of importance, studies, etc., that I felt might be useful. Soon I began to publish

EL HISPANO, a quarterly newsletter we sent out to all Hispanic pastors and leaders. Superintendents of Hispanic Conferences and individual churches gave me information that I felt would challenge our people, and the little paper was received with enthusiasm. It was sent out continuously during the seven years I worked in Evangelism USA.

We set up our Hispanic Ministries Counsel with the superintendents and leaders of Hispanics in different areas, and we later broadened that office to become Intercultural Ministries. Again I began to compile information that could be of benefit, and we formed our Intercultural Counsel composed of different ethnic groups. As a church, we needed to better understand each other, to interact, and to be challenged to reach out to different ethnic groups. During this time, I was given the opportunity to write often in our church periodicals. My intent was always to bring about a greater awareness of our multi-ethnicity as a nation and as a church. I must say that my life was greatly enriched as I rubbed shoulders with these leaders.

The General Conference of 1997 came, and I was in St. Louis. One morning along with everyone else I was standing with the elements of the Lord's Supper in my hands, when without any advanced notice, God spoke to me. "I'm changing your work," the Lord told me, "be prepared for a new ministry." Although the Lord didn't tell me what the change would be, nor when it would take place, the word from the Lord was so definite that I talked to my leaders about it.

Dr. Ronald Carpenter had just been elected to take over Evangelism USA, and I spoke to him. "You are just coming to the Department," I told him, "and you may have a person you want to put in the position I have been filling. If so, please feel free to make any change, because the Lord has told me He is changing my job." Dr. Carpenter asked me what I was going to do. "Well, I really don't know yet," I responded.

"Well, please stay on with me until you know, because I don't have anyone else for that job." I talked to out-going general superintendent of our denomination Bishop B. E. Underwood and in-coming Bishop James Leggett who had been the director of my work. I made the same statements, got the same questions, and received the same responses. Each one had accepted the fact that the Lord had spoken to me, but each one had encouraged me to stay where I was until the Lord gave me more specific directions. Don't ever forget that there is wisdom in the multitude of counselors. Don't be afraid to ask for counsel, because we sometimes are so close to our needs that we cannot see the road God is mapping out.

I also shared with the other workers in EVUSA, and everyone just accepted the fact that when the time came, the Lord would make things clear to me, and that they would know about it—everyone, that is, except Debbie Whipple. Debbie herself was a minister and was always interested in how God was moving. Every now and then, she asked me if God had said anything to me. One day she asked me the question again, and I said, "Well, what I would really like to see is…," and as I opened my mouth to speak, the Lord began to pour something new into my spirit, and what I expressed with my mouth was the work God wanted me to do.

I immediately went to my office and sat down to write. My pen seemed to flow over the paper almost automatically and without having to do a lot of thinking. I wanted to:

- Find some location where I could begin a Hispanic congregation.

- Call it *Centro de Celebration* (Celebration Center).

- Give the Hispanics of Oklahoma City a place to worship in their own language. It would not be bilingual from up front, because I was zealous that the young people not lose their native tongue. They will naturally become bilingual because of their friends at church and school—if they keep their native tongue!

- Provide earphones and translation into English for those who might come and need them.

- Offer theological studies and on-the-job training.

- Train people to become leaders and pastors as well as for local ministry.

- Involve children, not only in a children's church, but also in the regular worship services—especially in praise and worship.

I asked for an audience with Dr. Carpenter and he said, "EVUSA will help you get started." I talked to Dr. Owen Weston, our director of church planting, and we started working together. I had to project such things as location, when to begin, my target audience, financing, etc.

"I know just the place for you to begin," Superintendent James McDowell said. "Talk to Rev. John Youell," and I did.

"You can have your services on Sunday and Thursday nights at our church," he said, "and, yes, if you want to have your theological studies on Sunday morning, you can do that upstairs while we have service in the sanctuary." They gave me an office, and we went to work! We were in the middle of a Hispanic neighborhood at South Agnew and Southwest Twenty–Sixth Street. (Incidentally, my father had pastored the church at this location when I was in grade school, and I had attended Jackson Jr. High, which was just behind us.)

Our first activity was to show the "Jesus" film and to end with a snack time. Rev. Nicolas Becerra, pastor of *Centro Misionero Emanuel* (Emmanuel Missionary Center), and his congregation helped us that night. We didn't have many from the community, so I was very grateful to Brother Becerra for helping us with the music and to swell our attendance that night. We announced the first regular service for the following night. We were just a hand-full: Philip, my son, would play the guitar for us; Elí Velazquez who was interested in being a part of the church plant; Linda Stanberry a bilingual returned missionary; and two ladies from the English-speaking church, along with me. The next Sunday Pablo and Paz Gonzalez came and Carlos and Esther Aguilar plus members of their family swelled our group. Little by little, people were added to our number, but others who came moved on.

Summer arrived and people started leaving for vacation—especially to Mexico. One Sunday night we had the sum total of three! Brother Elí, Philip, and myself. My biggest concern was that EVUSA and the local church had made great investments in our beginning. We could not fail! We held on; people returned from vacation; others joined us, and we never looked back! I wish I could mention all the names, but it would be impossible. We continued to grow, but not in strides.

Not too long after beginning our work, we started our Center for Theological Studies. Elí Velazquez, an excellent teacher, was vital to this project, and I taught, along with others like Mamerto Díaz who was with us for a while from Venezuela. These studies continued until the Evangelism Department (EVUSA) started our National Hispanic Training Institute. The training on the local level, however, has continued in the area of preparation for local goals of evangelism.

The Acevedo family came and started *Grupo Sion,* and our children with their little flags became an integral part of worship at Celebration Center. The Lord brought Leticia Olmos to direct our worship, and she worked with our team of musicians—my son Philip, Carlos Obando—who came not long afterward, and others who came and went. God sent us Jaime and María Garcia and Misael Lucano to work with the children and youth. (These three are now working as missionaries outside the U.S.) These were ministries that had been a part of my vision for our church from the beginning.

The building where we worshipped was for sale, but I didn't feel that our church was strong enough to buy the property, and for some reason or other, I didn't feel it was exactly the place where we would be permanently located. The church sold, and on Easter Sunday, we had our first service in a new location. We were exactly two and one-half years old that Sunday.

Rev. Darryl Manning at Central Church opened his doors to us. My husband and I had pastored this church in the 1960s and the church had bought that property while we were with them. We would have the same options for services as with Rev. Youell. There would be a place for our Sunday morning studies and an office for me, as well as our services at the same times. God is *so* good—and so are people! We were now about seven miles from our previous location, and there were not nearly so many Hispanics around us. But strangely enough, we began a greater rhythm of growth. Hispanics in the area wanted to worship with us because our church was in their neighborhood. Little by little, the Lord added to the church, some by conversion, some by people who had no church home at that time, and immigrants God brought from different Latin American countries.

One of our principle goals by this time became to find church property. I continually had my eyes open looking for the place God had reserved for us. I was driving along Northwest Tenth Street one day with a lady who lived in that area, and I mentioned something I never told anyone else at that time. "I have just had sort of a flash of the church we are supposed to have," I told her. "It will have columns, sort of like that bank building there, but not quite. Of course, we could always add the columns! We could even put them on an industrial building!"

Later we were to have our Easter family retreat at the conference campgrounds, and I went out ahead of time to make sure everything was ready for us. I was checking out some things with the property manager when he mentioned that some tables and things had come out of one of our churches that was for sale. "Which church?" I asked, immediately interested.

"The original Muse Memorial property," he said, "but you don't want that! You'd need $100,000 to get into it plus your loan, and then it would probably take another $100,000 to fix it up. It is really a very big mess! I also think it is already under an option to buy."

I didn't have time to think too much about the property at that time since I was very much involved in the retreat that Friday evening and all day Saturday—then there were the Easter services on Sunday. Monday was supposed to be my day off, and I needed to get away. I got up early and made the three-hour trip to visit my sisters, Betty and Gertrude. I was tired, but I have always been able to relax as I drive, and I tried to do just that—putting out of mind anything that would keep me from the rest I needed. The next day as I returned, however, I began to seriously talk to the Lord. The Muse property was a historical, landmark building in our denomination. It was right across the street from where my husband and I, as well as my children, had gone to college. My daughter, Kathy, and her husband Gary, had married in that church edifice, as had many other couples of the church and college.

"Lord, you know I have been looking for the building you have for us. It seems incredible that we could have that property with its circular auditorium, its kitchen and gymnasium facilities, its offices and classroom space, and yes, its graceful columns out front! I need to hear from you, Lord! I need to know if that is the place you want us to have. It seems almost impossible." But the Lord answered me back!

"If you can believe, nothing, *nothing, NOTHING* is impossible." I felt I had the Lord's attention, and we continued our conversation!

"Well, Lord, it seems it is already under option for someone outside the denomination to buy, but if we are to have it, I know you can work it out."

Again the Lord came back with the words. "All things, *all things, ALL THINGS* are possible, if you can believe!" What could I say?

"Lord, $100,000 is an awful lot of money and then there will be a loan besides that." Again the Lord answered me back. "I am the source of everything you need!"

The miles had slipped by, and I had almost reached the exit for our Conference offices. I tried to call the superintendent to see if he was there, but the battery on my cell phone was down, so I drove on in to the property. Yes! He was there.

"Well, you just caught me," Brother McDowell said. "I'll be leaving in just a little bit and will be out of town for a while." Wow! God is never off on His timing, is He?

I must tell you that I was simply trembling under the power of the Holy Spirit as I sat down, and all I could say was, "Tell me about the Muse property." He told me the story without embellishments. The organ and the sound system had been removed. The place would demand a huge clean up and a revision of everything, especially the plumbing. There had been water damage and the carpet in the entrance had been pulled up, but there was supposed to be some insurance money if we replaced the carpet. Yes, the property was under option for a church outside the denomination to buy. They had been unable to get a loan, and the conference had just extended their option for three more months! If we did buy it, we would need $100,000 to clear the debts against the church and then take up the loan on it—this was because of the tremendous debts the previous congregation had left that had to be assumed by the conference. "I believe that is the property the Lord wants us to have," I told Brother McDowell.

"Well, then the Lord will work it all out," he said. We went to see the property, and indeed, it was a mess. One of the back columns had been hit and was in sad need of repair. But nothing actually looked impossible to me. *It will take a lot of work,* I thought.

Then the Lord seemed to say, "But I have given you people who will help you *do* it!"

I immediately talked to my sister and her husband, Evelyn and Hollis Thurmond. They knew the property and wanted me to have it. They offered me a generous gift on the property. "Start raising the money," they said, "and we'll stand behind you while it comes in. Tell Brother McDowell not to give those people another extension—that the conference already has a buyer. You can buy it." I was so sure of the word I had from the Lord that I began to write letters; at first to good friends and family members, then later to those to whom the property meant a great deal. They were scattered from the West Coast to the East and from the North to the South. That had been their church home or their church while studying at college. They had been married there or had dedicated their babies in those facilities. They would be interested in keeping the property as the landmark that it had always been…and the money began to come in. A thousand here…a hundred there…twenty-five…two hundred.

"Have you contacted Bill Anderson?" my daughter asked. Well, I hadn't looked up his address yet. "Well, get it," she said. "He will want to know what you are doing." And he did. Bill had pastored that congregation for twenty years. He had added the gym, designed, and built the new sanctuary that by now was about thirty years old. He and his father, Rev. W.J. Anderson, had literally poured themselves into the construction of that facility. Bill and his wife, Bette, immediately sent me a check for $1,000, and they continued to send that amount month after month. They later gave us their RV, which we sold for $22,500. Thank you, Bill and Bette! They also continued their support after that time.

The local people gave in amounts of $1,000, $500, $200, $100. The young people also gave and the children. "How could this teenager possibly give $75?" I asked her parents.

"She made that money baby-sitting," they told me. As time passed, I saw those who sacrificed the most blessed to purchase their own homes! One by one, many of them moved from apartments into their own properties! God always blesses those who bless Him and His work.

I had stuck my neck out, but God didn't let me down. Finally, I was informed that the people who had wanted to buy the property again had not been able to raise the money. "You can buy it," they said! We had the money ready. Evelyn and Hollis Thurmond stood behind me on what we lacked to reach the $100,000. (They gave us that loan without interest, and we have paid $1,000 every month on it in addition to the payment on our principle loan, and now that loan to them has been cancelled. We are looking forward to the day when the property will be completely free of debt!) It seems there were things the conference itself had to do to clear up details on the property, but since we were all in the same denomination, we had faith, and while things were being taken care of, we were allowed to begin work and clean-up on the property.

From the first week in June until the middle of October, our people were at 4725 Northwest Tenth Street at work. Huge truckloads of trash were hauled off. New problems were always resurfacing as we worked. When we repaired one thing, another seemed to pop up. My sister Evelyn came to help us price things for a gym sale—we hoped to be able to get rid of some of the stuff without junking it! The ladies had worked diligently to put things on tables and sort them out. It was then that Evelyn realized the enormity of the task we had taken on. I walked through the building showing it to Bob Cramp, my brother-in-law.

"When the Lord told you to get this property, did He know how old you were?" Bob and I were the same age, so *he* knew.

"Yes, the Lord knew," I said, "and that is the reason He is giving us such wonderful help."

I visited different businesses with a notebook I had prepared. It told just a little of our history and had pictures of the churches where we had been and of the project we were undertaking as we restored the property we were buying. Ana Maria and Rosario wanted to make visits, too, and did they ever come back rejoicing! They had been able to get several contributions, but there was a special one! A man had looked at my picture and the picture of the church. "I know that lady," he said, "she is a missionary. And I know that church." I'll give you 100 gallons of paint!" Other businesses gave us paint, plumbing, bathroom equipment, etc.

What might have been impossible under some circumstances became possible with God and us together. We had people who served as maintenance managers in apartment complexes and others who had had experience in their own homes. They knew how to paint, repair walls, do plumbing, and fix bathrooms! We went to work with a will, and I shall never cease to praise the Lord for the unfailing work of the people who, week after week and month after month, just stayed right with me to make it possible for us to move in. We replaced the beautiful purple carpet that had to be special-dyed (that would have been impossible without the insurance money), checked all the wiring and lighting (replacing much of it), repaired walls with new sheetrock, and painted everything. But every day was like a fiesta! We brought food and soft drinks, and the kids played in the sand of the playground! They, too, were a precious part of our time together.

There were times of near disaster—like one day when I arrived to find water spewing out of a pipe next to the ladies' lounge. I couldn't find the cut off, but I managed to call a brother who had been helping with the plumbing, and he was on his way to answer my distress call. Meanwhile, I stood there trying to hold down the leak. As a result, I got wet from head to toe. My hair was plastered to my head, and my clothes hung on me like a wet wash. I'm sure I probably looked half-drowned! We had just managed to get the water cut off, when in the middle of everything, the man donating the paint arrived! There was no way I could have looked like the person he had in seen in the picture! I could only give thanks to the Lord and rejoice, however, because I had reached the building just in time to keep it from being flooded with water!

It was exactly five years from the time we started the church to the time we had our opening service in our permanent place of worship. My son Paul was with me for a time of vacation; he was everywhere, helping with the yard clean-up, the carpet, and dozens of other things right along with the rest of the church people. We had our opening service on a Sunday afternoon, and it was bilingual in order to invite people who had shared with us in the purchase and restoration process. Over two hundred people were present, and we were grateful to the many people from the original Muse Congregation (now River of Life) who expressed their gratefulness to us for restoring a landmark edifice that had meant so much to them in their Christian experience.

Our sanctuary will seat 750 people with its balcony, and to date we are still concentrating on filling the lower level that will seat about 350. Our average attendance was about 125, and we sort of felt that we were rattling around in it (especially when the children left for their service!) Of course, the numbers would swell for special occasions, and then drop back down. It is not easy to build a solid foundation of truly committed people.

Early in the New Year, I walked into the sanctuary, and my heart was moved by the capacity of our sanctuary. I began one of my conversations with the Lord. "You know, Lord, I really didn't ask for a sanctuary this big, but this is what you have given us. Everything is so clean and renewed, and we have the space we need to carry out all we feel called to do. But I'm sure you didn't give this to us just to be a small congregation. You had a purpose in giving us this particular facility, and if we fill this place, we are going to have to grow!" The more I thought about it, the more I realized that we would not be able to fulfill God's will for us in our building if we just carried on as usual. If we just continued to do what we were doing, we would get the same results. Traditional methods would not bring us to the fullness of God's will!

Kathy and Gary came back from Spain, and we began to talk about a cell-group ministry. They had been involved in Venezuela, and the Lord had greatly blessed there. I began to read and study cell-group ministry again and took a trip to Bogotá, Colombia, to visit a convention hosted by Cesar Castellanos. I came back enthused, and we began to work toward new goals to win, establish, disciple, and send believers to reach the lost.

When we win a new person to the Lord, we must establish that person in the church through teaching the basics of the new life in Christ. Our next step for new people is a retreat (called an Encounter) emphasizing inner holiness, the baptism of the Holy Spirit, and the vision of the church. The discipleship phase of the program is to equip that person in the Word; teaching them how to be a good leader and how to establish and carry on a cell ministry. It is hoped that each one will be a part of a small group and will hopefully train to become the leader of a cell.

What I really wanted was the mobilization of every Christian in the action of winning and establishing people in the work of the church. I set a new theme for our work: "Every believer a mobilizing disciple!" We emphasize the fact that when Jesus said, "Come ye after me, and I will make you fishers of men," that meant winning souls! Our basic verse in the Bible is Matthew 28:19–20. "Go ye therefore and teach (disciple) all nations, baptizing them in the name of the Father and of the Son and of the Holy Spirit, teaching them to observe all things whatsoever I have commanded you, and behold I am with you always, even unto the end of the age." There was the whole program: win, establish, disciple, and go (send)!

Kathy's messages to the church were challenging. "Many people in our pews are just observers," she said. "We have to make a decision to be changed from spectators to conquerors—from receivers to givers." I began to focus my preaching ministry on this challenge, and I was probably challenged more than anyone else. Kathy and Gary helped me with our first Encounter, and God blessed by filling the people with the Holy Spirit. We began an early morning prayer (5:00–9:00 a.m.), and although it was not always well attended, I was always there and Kathy was with me as long as she was in the States. We carried on this ministry for several months.

By faith, I counted as already done that which the physical eye could not see. I prayed over the entire building, especially the sanctuary. I prayed over the empty pews. I told the people I saw by faith, "I'm so glad you have come today. God is here to meet your need. Just reach out and touch Him." From section to section of those empty pews of imaginary people I declared God's blessings—spiritual blessings, material and financial blessings, physical blessings, blessings on the home, on the job, at school, and in the church. I went up the stairs to the balcony, and I spoke to the people I saw there through the eye of faith. "God has brought you here for a reason. He wants to bless you! He is the answer to all your needs! Reach out and touch Him today!" I declared to all of them, "You are not just a spectator! You are a conqueror! You are an overcomer! You are a soul-winner!"

We began training those who were catching the vision. I realized that I did not embrace this vision overnight, and I understood those who did not catch on immediately. With time, we identified leaders, and they began to form cells. Some were successful and seemed to have a knack for reaching the lost. Others did not win so very quickly, but their work was fruitful. Some cells were made up mostly of church people who were not really reaching the lost. We had leaders who persisted and saw their cells grow, while others sort of lost interest and saw their cells fall apart. I was able to identify some common problems.

- If a group reaches an attendance of twenty committed adults without dividing, it will start to decline. It should divide after reaching a group of twelve committed people. The cell will not *multiply* until the cell divides, and there are two cells instead of one. Each cell leader will then work toward growing their cells and dividing them again. They will either multiply and divide or decline!

- Another problem is when the members of the group are not really dedicated to the growth of the cell. Every member must be committed to reaching the lost. Some might say they aren't growing because the leader or the host doesn't get out and bring in new people, but getting new people to the cell is the commitment of each member of the group—not just of the leader or host!

- Then there are the groups that just become another little church "service," but in reality, the church doesn't need more "services." It has to trim back extra activities in order to get the cell ministry going and to cut unnecessary departmental or group activity. If new people are not won, the group is not fulfilling its purpose for existence. The group was born to win the lost and to grow, and principally to develop new leaders.

- The work will grow only as cell leaders develop new leaders in order to divide when the proper time comes. The work can grow only to the extent that new leaders are formed.

At this time, *Centro de Celebración* has in action a number of cells that are bringing growth, but we are still a church in transition. God gave me a vision in 1960 and I have not been disobedient to that heavenly vision. I have ministered in Central and South America just as He showed me that I would, and He has held me in the hollow of His hand as I have traveled to many different nations of the world: Europe, Asia, the Near East, Latin America, and North Africa. If I can mobilize the believers of our Celebration Center to become multiplying disciples, however, I may well set into motion one of the greatest accomplishments of my ministry. We are on our way, but we have not yet arrived. For some a cell group is just a little too much work. Some say that the method will work in Latin America, but the people of the U.S. are just "too busy." But churches in this country are now proving that to be untrue. I challenge these objections! As Christians, we must never become too busy to be what God called us to be—fishers of men—people who are winning and making disciples of others to reach the lost and dying for Christ.

Impossible? *Nothing* is impossible! Not enough money? Our God is the owner of this earth and everything in it! *He* is the Source of all we need! Every difficulty is just a stepping-stone to success! Every seed we plant holds in itself the capacity to become a forest! Life is a Great Adventure! Never forget it, and it gets more exciting the closer we get to the end. Thanks for coming along!

Benediction

To bless others is a primary biblical concept. God blesses us, and we are to bless Him and also other people. Our words of blessing upon our families can be prophetic, and our children may either consciously or unconsciously work toward their fulfillment. When Isaac mistakenly blessed Jacob instead of Esau, he could not recall his words. As spoken words they had become history, and God would fulfill them. Jacob was a very old man when Joseph brought his two sons to him for blessing. Joseph put Manasseh on Jacob's right hand so that he would give him the blessing of the firstborn, but Jacob astutely crossed his hands and blessed Ephraim above Manasseh. (He must have remembered his own concern over being the second in line!) Before he died, Jacob gathered his sons around him, called out the name of each one of them, and blessed them. According to Old Testament concepts, the spoken word had power in itself to fulfill what had been declared.

"God bless you," or "May God continue to bless you," is the common way we greet people of the church in Latin culture. When we bless people, we should consider that God will in his own way fulfill his Word and bring about that blessing!

As I bring this story to its conclusion, I can think of no better way to end it than by blessing you in the name of the Lord!

- To my four children, their spouses and children…

- To each of my grandchildren and great grandchildren…

- To my sisters, my brother, and my one brother-in-law who is still with us, and to their children and grandchildren…

- To my spiritual sons and daughters in Christ who have come to be saved or blessed under my ministry…

- To all of those faithful people who have worked alongside me in the ministry–here in the United States and in the regions beyond…

- To those of you who do not know me personally, but you have read this story and have been blessed in some way…I bless you!

I bless you in the name of the Father, and of the Son, and of the Holy Spirit! I declare that since you have decided to be a true disciple of the Lord by following in his footsteps, your ministry is to reach the lost, to proclaim a life of victory and holiness for the believer, and of the fullness of the Spirit toward those who by faith will reach out and receive. I declare for you a life of authority! You are seated with Christ in heavenly places. What is under the feet of Christ is under *your* feet, because in Him you live, move, and have your being. You are in Him, and He is in you! And *these signs* will follow you as you believe: you will speak with new tongues, you will cast out demons; you will lay your hands on the sick and they will recover!

I pray upon you blessings of material prosperity as you follow the Lord by generously giving to Him of your tithes and offerings. You are blessed, because God promised you that if you would give to Him, he would open the windows of heaven and pour abundant blessings out upon you. He also said he would rebuke the devourer! I pray upon you spiritual blessings as you seek the Lord, for He is found of those who seek him. I bless you in your social life as you interact with others and witness to them of God's grace and glory. I bless you with physical health as you exercise and eat right. I declare that Jesus carried your pains and sicknesses to the cross, and that you are free to follow Him in health. I rebuke every sickness that would try to attach itself to you, and I declare God's blessing of health upon you as you work for Him. I cancel out, in the name of Jesus, every scheme that the enemy would try to plot against you.

I speak protection for those who live in areas restricted to the Gospel. You may not be openly able to witness for the Lord, and my heart beats for you. I bless you with God's peace that passes all understanding, and I pray that you will be faithful in all the circumstances of this life.

You took your first step on Life's Great Adventure when you made your decision to receive Christ as Lord of your Life. You have embraced Him, and now you will step out and share with others! You are not just a bench warmer in the church! You are not just a receiver! You are an over-comer! You are more than a conqueror in Christ! May you walk in victory as you walk in Christ. Life with Him is truly a life of Great Adventure! Thanks for making this journey with me. It's been a joy to have you travel along.